BROAD LEYS

BY CFA VOYSEY

THE CREATION, LIFE AND TIMES
OF AN ARTS AND CRAFTS HOUSE

HOME TO
**WINDERMERE MOTOR
BOAT RACING CLUB**

MATTHEW HYDE

Broad Leys; The creation, life and times of an Arts and Crafts house.
Copyright © 2013. Windermere Motor Boat Racing Club.

All rights reserved. No other part of this book, including photographs, may be reproduced in any form or by any electronic or mechanical means including information storage and retrieval systems without permission in writing from the publisher, except by a reviewer, who may quote brief passages in a review.

Images used with thanks to:
Victoria & Albert Museum, Windermere Steamboat Museum, Abbot Hall, Lakeland Arts Trust, The National Trust, University of Leeds Library Special Collection, Kendal Archive Centre, Windermere Golf Club, Malcolm Casson Photography, Shirley Schofield, Verlie McCann, Currer Briggs family, MacIver family & Members of WMBRC.

Although every precaution has been taken in the preparation of this book, the publisher and author assume no responsibility for errors or omissions. Neither is any liability assumed for damages resulting from the use of this information contained herein. Attempts have been made to identify all the images used in this book, however, despite best efforts, some images remain untraceable.

Published by Compass Publishing.
Designed and Set by Fullpoint Design. T: 015394 47100.
Printed in the United Kingdom by Paragon Printing. T:0161 477 6645.

ISBN 978-1-907308-92-5
First Edition printed 2013 in the United Kingdom.
A catalogue record for this book is available from the British Library

CONTENTS

FOREWORD

THERE WAS A ROAR IN THE
DISTANCE, GETTING RAPIDLY
LOUDER. A SPLASH OF WHITE
SHOWED BEYOND THE ISLAND
NEAR THE STEAMER. IT SEEMED TO
SLIDE OVER THE WATER NEARER
AND NEARER. IT WAS A FAST
MOTOR BOAT, MUCH FASTER THAN
THE STEAMER AND HUNDREDS OF
TIMES LOUDER. IT ROARED UP THE
LAKE A HUNDRED YARDS AWAY
AND SOON DISAPPEARED ASTERN.

When the Currer Briggs family generously donated their collection of photographs of the interior of Broad Leys and its gardens, Peter White, at that time Chairman of House of Windermere Motor Boat Racing Club, quickly realised their significance and potential. Designed by the renowned Arts and Crafts architect C.F.A.Voysey at the turn of the 19th century, Broad Leys was ground breaking in its time.

The photographs taken by photographer and father of Beatrix Potter, Rupert Potter, in the early 1900s, are a superb and unique record of the interiors and furnishings of the time. Peter White was also aware of the vast archive of information in the attic at Broad Leys and felt that this also needed to be seen by a wider audience. Having approached a fellow WMBRC member Helen Pugh to catalogue the archival material, he then came to the inevitable conclusion that "there was a story to be told".

Matthew Hyde, architectural historian, who had already worked in this area and has an interest in Arts and Crafts houses was asked to write this story.

As Broad Leys has been the home of Windermere Motor Boat Racing Club since 1951, the history of racing at the club also needed a voice. WMBRC is privileged to have Broad Leys as its home but equally were it not for the financial support the club provides, the house might not have been preserved in its present state.

Hence this book seeks to tell the story of the history of Broad Leys, its owners, its many distinguished visitors including Beatrix Potter, Hardwick Rawnsley (founder member of The National Trust), Donald Campbell and even the Belgian detective of Agatha Christie fame Hercule Poirot, together with the intertwining history of racing at WMBRC.

The members of the general committee have generously approved and supported the funding of this book.

We hope that Voysey's legacy at Broad Leys will be appreciated by all who read it.

LEFT   The terrace at Broad Leys, today

ACKNOWLEDGEMENTS

'MR VOYSEY'S SIMPLICITY OF MANNER, HIS AIM TO USE HONEST MATERIALS IN A STRAIGHTFORWARD WAY, HIS OCCASIONAL TOUCHES OF HUMOUR, SUCH AS APPEAR EVEN IN HIS MOST IMPORTANT WORKS - ALL THESE ARE THE OPEN EXPRESSION OF THE MAN AS WELL AS THE ARCHITECT.'

STUDIO MAGAZINE
VOL 9 1896.

Many people have helped with the writing of this book. Special thanks are due to Peter White who commissioned the book on behalf of the Windermere Motor Boat Racing Club, and who has shared his long experience of motorboat racing as well as his enthusiasm for the club and Voysey's architecture.

My grateful thanks to Helen Pugh, archivist and co-researcher, who was my introduction to the job and whose help and support throughout have been invaluable.

To the many WMBRC members who have talked to Helen and myself, and helped with pictures; among others Richard Solomon, Robin Brown (dec.), Ted Walsh, Martyn Lewis, Chris Loney, Peter Radcliffe, Harry Leung and Rowan Ashworth in the Lodge.

Thanks also to Margaret Reid at the Windermere Steamboat Museum, Verlie McCann at the Leeds Children's Holiday Camp, Shirley Schofield at Whitwood, Kathy Haslam, ex-curator of Blackwell, and Teddy Pattinson of Gossel Ridding.

Special thanks to current members of the Currer-Briggs family for their help with information and photographs.

And finally, to Broad Leys itself and the staff who have made me so welcome there.

MATTHEW HYDE

LEFT   Broad Leys main entrance

A VILLA IN THE ENGLISH LAKES

SOME OF THE HOUSES BUILT THEN ACHIEVED A PERFECTION NEVER SEEN BEFORE AND NEVER EQUALLED SINCE

According to Wordsworth, the very first house built in the Lake District for the sake of the landscape was Belle Isle, the temple like house on an island in the middle of Windermere. That was in the 1770s, when the beauty of the Lakes was just beginning to be appreciated by the world at large. Others soon followed and by 1900 the long eastern shore of Windermere, the largest of the lakes as well as the easiest one to reach, was strung with a necklace of delicious villas, each set in its choice garden and commanding its own particular view of lake and fell.

The railways have never really penetrated the Lake District, thanks partly to the terrain but also to fierce opposition by preservationists, not least of them Wordsworth himself. The only really handy railhead was at Windermere, established in 1847. This made weekly or even daily travel to Manchester from a lakeside villa feasible. Conversely, the railway opened up the Lakes, especially Windermere, to day trippers who flooded in on Sundays and Bank Holidays.

The years around 1900 saw a revolution in the domestic arts, the art of building and furnishing a beautiful home. Britain was in many ways at its peak, the centre of a great empire, an international powerhouse of industry. But it was also ready for something new. The long reign of Queen Victoria was finally nearing its end; she died on the 25th January 1901. Here in Coniston the equally long lived Victorian sage, John Ruskin, died on the 20th January 1900.

Some of the houses built then achieved a perfection never seen before and never equalled since, embodying a whole set of beliefs derived from William Morris and Ruskin in the honesty of simple materials and the dignity and value of labour, as well as a delight in nature and the outdoor life. It was a particularly British, even English, phenomenon, though it had a world wide influence. We call it the Arts and Crafts Movement. Where Victorian houses had been fussy, oppressive, over designed, over engineered, and over stuffed with knick knacks, the Arts and Crafts house was clean and bright, comfortably proportioned and beautifully simple. Modern, yet harking back to an ideal of the pre-industrial age.

Among the Windermere villas the three which best encapsulate the Arts and Crafts ideal are Blackwell, Broad Leys and Moor Crag. All three were commissioned in about 1898 and all were finished

LEFT The terrace at Broad Leys in the early 1900s

by 1901. They are not far apart either, all being close to the old Westmorland / Lancashire border south of Bowness.

Blackwell, set high above the lake, was designed by M. H. Baillie Scott for Sir Edward Holt of Manchester, his wife Elizabeth and their five children. Holt (1849-1928), a brewer, was in many ways a typical wealthy offcomer. His father Joseph had lived next to the brewery, in Empire Street, Cheetham, but in 1861 he built a big and gloomy gothic mansion called Woodthorpe by Heaton Park - the house being converted into a Holts pub in 1955. Alderman and then twice Mayor of a proudly independent, confident, upwardly mobile city,

Edward Holt was rich, public spirited, progressive and practical. His philanthropy is remembered today in Manchester's Holt Radium Institute and Christie Hospital. The building in the 1890s of the Thirlmere dam and aqueduct epitomises the ambitions and confidence of the city and Holt's practical concern for public health and clean water. Blackwell was convenient for keeping an eye on the Thirlmere works, while providing for a much freer lifestyle than in Manchester. At the other end, Heaton Park itself was purchased by the City of Manchester in 1902, partly for the recreation of its citizens but partly to make a receiving reservoir for Lake District water.

BLACKWELL WAS CONVENIENT FOR KEEPING AN EYE ON THE THIRLMERE WORKS

BELOW Blackwell designed by M.H. Baillie Scott for Sir Edward Holt of Manchester

ABOVE Moor Crag designed by C.F.A Voysey for Manchester textile manufacturer J.W. Buckley

THE NEW HOUSES WERE NOT SUSTAINED BY THE WEALTH OF THE LAND. THEY WERE THERE BECAUSE OF ITS BEAUTY.

Moor Crag was designed by C.F.A. Voysey for J. W. Buckley, a Manchester textile manufacturer. He also had a big house in Altrincham, Westwood, which still stands. Dated 1873, it is built of a typically Victorian mix of materials: white brick with red brick highlights, tile hanging, and timber-framing. Moor Crag, with its beautifully designed cottage-like simplicity must have provided a marvellous relief from the cares and complications of Manchester.

Broad Leys, the subject of this book, was built by Voysey for Arthur and Helen Currer Briggs of Leeds.

The new houses were not sustained by the wealth of the land. They were there because of its beauty.

The money to build and maintain them was made elsewhere. The fortunes made from the dirty and despoiling industries of South Lancashire and Yorkshire were spent by the lucky few at the top of the pyramid on a choice villa and an idyllic life in the Lake District. The top of the middle class in fact, able to commission a house expressive of the simple life based on high ideals and cushioned by financial security. The aspiring middle class were newly affluent, newly cultured, and often represented the second generation of a classic clogs-to-clogs parabola. Father, starting at the bottom, makes a fortune in industrial Manchester, Bolton or Leeds by sheer hard graft, living over the shop or next to the mill. Son is sent to a good school and university, starts to look around, travels, indulges in philanthropy, and commissions an Arts and Crafts

house in the Lakes. Grandson enjoys Lakeland life so much that he takes his eye off the business. Income starts to slide. The city connection is lost, and sooner or later the Lake District villa will have to be sold.

Looking back, it was something of a golden age, with elegant steam launches taking stylishly dressed ladies and gentlemen from house party to house party, superb sailing yachts swooping down the lake on race days and happy children intrepidly

exploring the islands and woods before coming home for tea and hunks of cake. Perhaps.

Accounts of the great freeze in January 1895 bring back those days:

'Such a scene presented itself as can only be seen in some old Dutch city in mid-winter. The whole interspace between the land and the island was powdered white from the innumerable iron heels of the skaters. Here a pony with its jangling sleigh

THE WHOLE INTERSPACE BETWEEN THE LAND AND THE ISLAND WAS POWDERED WHITE FROM THE INNUMERABLE IRON HEELS OF THE SKATERS.

bells dashed along; there fond fathers pushed their little ones in perambulators. A hurdy gurdy man made music here, and yonder, on St Mary's Holme, a brass band blew its best, and risked frozen lips and frost bitten fingers in the process. Tea, one was reminded, was obtainable here; oranges were possible there. Presently a great boat sail was seen to belly to the wind and an iceboat slid past.'

Arthur Ransome had the great good fortune to be at school at Windermere in February 1895 at the time of the Great Frost, when for week after week the lake was frozen from end to end. Lessons became perfunctory. 'After breakfast, day after day,

provisions were placed on a big toboggan and we ran it down into Bowness when we tallied on to ropes astern of it to hold it back and prevent it from crashing into the hotel at the bottom. During those happy weeks we spent the whole day on the ice, leaving the steely lake only at dusk when fires were already burning and torches lit and our elders carried lanterns as they skated and shot about like fireflies. I saw a coach and four drive across the ice, and the roasting of an ox (I think) on Bowness Bay. Those weeks of clear ice with that background of snow covered, sunlit, blue shadowed hills were, forty years after, to give me a book called Winter Holiday for which I have a sort of tenderness.'

BOATING ON WINDERMERE

THE LAKE IS AND ALWAYS HAS BEEN A PUBLIC HIGHWAY, VITAL FOR BUSINESS, FOR PRACTICAL TRANSPORT, AND FOR PLEASURE.

Until the lakeside roads were improved it was the best way to get about. Boats are a central aspect of life. The lakeside houses are provided with handsome boathouses, sometimes quite elaborate, as at Fellfoot, Wray, Pullwoods, and Langdale Chase.

ABOVE   Langdale Chase Boathouse

LEFT   The steamboat *Dodo*
         (Courtesy of the MacIver family)

RIGHT   *On The Same Tack,* racing sailing boats on
         Windermere, 1890. *(Courtesy of Windermere
         Steamboat Museum)*

THE AGE OF SAIL

Serious racing is recorded as early as 1786, when Margaret regularly raced against Peggy; both boats still exist. Water Carnivals and Regattas were much enjoyed. They were jolly affairs, with competitions for fishing, men's and women's neat diving, rowing, pillow fights, hobby horse races, and decorated boats, finishing with a grand display of fireworks. Competition in the sailing races was fierce, especially when entrepreneurs from Manchester or Leeds came on the scene.

The first boats designed specifically for racing appeared in the 1860s, and with them the need for rules. The Windermere Sailing Club was formed in 1860 to determine handicaps and lay down a fair set of racing rules. Prime movers in its genesis were competitive gentlemen from industrial Lancashire who had acquired lakeside properties. Colonel Ridehalgh, originally from Prestwich in Manchester, bought Fellfoot in 1859. Joseph Bridson, of Bolton, took various properties including Belle Isle, and then built Bryerswood at Sawrey in 1886. His architect there was R. Knill Freeman also from Bolton and the house, though employing alien timber-framing, was an interesting precursor of the Arts and Crafts. Racing around the turn of the century must have presented one of the most beautiful and spectacular sights the lake has ever seen. The Windermere yachts with their graceful lines, long bowsprits and towering gaff topsails were superb, reaching a peak of beauty, design and craftsmanship with the magnificent 22 foot racing yachts of 1897. Twenty six of them were built by the boatbuilders in Bowness Bay; Shepherds, Brockbanks, and Borwick & Son, including Ibis in 1904 for Joseph Holt of Blackwell, but they were a rich man's prerogative. The more modest Windermere class 17 footers, introduced in 1904, still race.

BELOW Following the yacht race
(Courtesy of Windermere Steamboat Museum, Donald Potts Collection)

WINDERMERE REGATTA

Parsonage Bay and Rectory Farm Field,

Saturday, Sept. 11th, 1926, at 2 p.m.

President : A. CRABTREE, ESQ., J.P.
Hon. Treas.: MR. A. H. ROBINSON.
Hon. Secs.: MR. G. E. BORWICK, Cockshott, Bowness.
MR. W. J. McVEY, F.A.I., Royal Square.

Prizes will be distributed on the Field by Mrs. A. CRABTREE
at the conclusion of Event No. 23.

Selections of Music by the Windermere
Town Band.

Refreshments will be provided on the Field at reasonable charges.

PRICE 2d.

WATER CARNIVALS AND REGATTAS WERE MUCH ENJOYED. THEY WERE JOLLY AFFAIRS, WITH COMPETITIONS FOR FISHING, MEN'S AND WOMEN'S NEAT DIVING, ROWING, PILLOW FIGHTS, HOBBY HORSE RACES, AND DECORATED BOATS, FINISHING WITH A GRAND DISPLAY OF FIREWORKS.

LEFT   Windermere Regatta Flyer, 1926
ABOVE   On the starting line, 1890
         (Courtesy of Windermere Steamboat Museum)

ABOVE Mr Bowler's Boat *(Courtesy of Windermere Steamboat Museum)*
BELOW *Elfin* at speed *(Courtesy of Windermere Steamboat Museum)*

ABOVE German Kaiser Wilhelm II disembarking from *Maru* on the Wanlass Howe jetty during his visit in 1895 escorted by the Earl of Lonsdale with *Dodo*, *Elfin* and *Tern* seen in the background.
(Courtesy of the MacIver family)

STEAM.

Mechanical power came to the lake with the launching in 1845 of the 75-ft paddle-steamer Lady of the Lake. This 'elegant steam yacht' offered twice-daily trips between Newby Bridge and Ambleside at a cost of 3/-. Such was her success that she was followed in 1846 by a sister ship, Lord of the Isles and the Teal, built in 1890.

Just a year after the first steamer, in 1847, the arrival of the railway revolutionised access to the Lakes.

Already the impulse for progress and modernisation was opposed by a powerful movement for preservation and the status quo. There was some opposition to the smoke and commotion of the steamers, but the railway faced fierce condemnation. Headed by Wordsworth himself, the opposition stopped the railway from going any further than the first terminus at Birthwaite, a good two miles up from the lake. So here in due course the railway town of Windermere sprung up.

In about 1850 Charles Fildes built the paddler Fairy Queen, and his brother Alfred built the little screw steamer Dolly. The Fildes brothers were from Manchester but had a house near Sawrey. After many adventures Dolly survives. She was salvaged from Ullswater in 1962, transported back to Windermere, and restored to steaming order by G.H. Pattinson.

A famous private steam launch, also preserved (though in poor condition), was the Esperance, built for W.H. Schneider of Belsfield. Schneider was a pioneer prospector for the pure iron ore of Furness, but is best remembered today for what must be the most stylish commute ever. Every morning, preceded by his butler with the breakfast tray, he would make his way from his Italianate villa, Belsfield, down the lawn to the jetty. A

ABOVE Col. Ridehalgh's steam yacht of 1859, also Fairy Queen

LEFT Sladen's *Phantom*

BELOW *Linnet*

ABOVE Afternoon tea on *Britannia*
(*Courtesy of Windermere Steamboat Museum*)

BELOW *Britannia* during Queen Victoria jubilee
celebrations on Windermere 1887.

hearty silver service breakfast was partaken on board Esperance as she steamed down the lake. A special train awaited at Lakeside to speed him to Barrow, while with a secretary he began the day's business. But even Esperance was outshone by Col. Ridehalgh's magnificent 110-foot Britannia, launched in 1879, the ultimate in elegant grandeur. She was broken up in 1916 (the saloon rooflight was found in 1979 doing duty in Barrow as a greenhouse), but Ridehalgh's boatyard at Fellfoot, a proper dockyard complex in miniature, survives complete and can be visited. More typical was the beautiful launch Branksome, built in 1896 for Mrs. Howarth of Langdale Chase. Branksome (originally Lily) is perhaps the most luxurious boat ever to sail on Windermere. Built by Brockbanks of Bowness from entire 51ft planks of teak, she has a walnut panelled saloon with velvet upholstery and leather seats, galley, a WC and solid marble washbasin, and of course a Windermere kettle which boils a gallon of water in 10 seconds. The splendid boathouse at Langdale Chase was specifically built for her.

ELECTRIC POWER

As early as 1898 electricity was harnessed to drive the 32 foot launch Swallow, built by Shepherd & Borwick's for William Warburton of Belle Grange, near Wray, and Manchester. A water driven generator kept the acid accumulators charged up. By 1900 G.H. Pattinson, who among his other enterprises had helped pioneer the electricity supply in Windermere, was keeping three electric boats at Storrs. One was always fully charged for instant use; a steam launch might need an hour to raise steam before it could be used.

The pleasure of an electric boat is silent and effortless travel, but the batteries are always a problem: acid leakage then, danger of explosion now.

ABOVE The Warburtons on the electric launch *Swallow* *(Courtesy of Windermere Steamboat Museum, from the Reverend Kemble of Wray Collection)*

BORWICKS (WINDERMERE) LTD
BOATBUILDERS
&
ENGINEERS
WINDERMERE

WATERBIRD.

The first serious public tussle over noise and nuisance on the lake came in 1911 not over a boat but over an aeroplane. The story starts in the early days of manned flight with a rivalry between Captain Edward Wakefield and Oscar Gnosspelius to build a successful amphibious aircraft. This was only two years after Louis Blériot had made the first cross-channel flight. On the 25th November 1911 Gnosspelius No 2 took off successfully, but a wingtip trailed in the water and the plane flipped over. On the same day Wakefield's Waterbird, piloted by H. Stanley-Adams (who was unaware of the accident), took off, flew down the lake, turned and came back to a safe landing. This was a first for Britain, if not Europe. Later that day a second successful flight was photographed by Frank Herbert.

Gnosspelius incidentally exemplifies the multiple links of family and friendship in our story. One of the founder members of the Motor Boat Club, he married Barbara Collingwood, daughter of W.G. Collingwood the author, artist, archaeologist and friend of Ruskin. Their daughter Dorothy married Ernest Altounyan and their four children are the Swallows of Arthur Ransome's stories.

BELOW *Waterbird* in flight over Windermere

Waterbird was a flimsy sticks and string biplane with a pusher engine (50 h.p. Gnome rotary) and propellor behind the pilot. It was built by A. V. Roe (Avro) of Manchester, tested at Brooklands, and then converted for water by Borwicks of Bowness. The float design was critical in order that the aeroplane could 'unstick' for take off - the same problem faced by designers of planing boats from Uffa Fox to Donald Campbell.

Waterbird made sixty flights in the first month or so, and on December 7th 1911 Stanley-Adams droned the whole length of the lake at a speed of about 40 m.p.h. The new development did not please everybody. Indeed if one can imagine the quietness and peace of the lake in 1911 it must have been very intrusive. Beatrix Potter wrote from Sawrey to Country Life and the Times: 'a more inappropriate place for experimenting with flying machines could scarcely be chosen'. She was backed by the great campaigner Hardwicke Rawnsley.

In the event nature took its course; a storm early in 1912 blew down the hangar at Cockshott, and the plane was damaged beyond repair. After experimenting with a second plane called Waterhen the war put an end to the affair.

Incidentally, in 1927 Beatrix Potter helped the National Trust to buy and preserve Cockshott Point.

"A MORE INAPPROPRATE PLACE FOR EXPERIMENTING WITH FLYING MACHINES COULD SCARELY BE CHOSEN"
BEATRIX POTTER, 1911

BELOW *Waterbird* on Windermere

ABOVE An early power boat, 1898

(Courtesy of Windermere Steamboat Museum)

ONCE MOTOR BOATS HAD
DEVELOPED TO THIS STAGE IT DID
NOT TAKE LONG FOR SOME OF
THOSE INVOLVED TO MEET AND
DECIDE TO FORM A MOTOR BOAT
CLUB.

POWERBOATS.

The power and efficiency of internal combustion engines was greatly improved during the Great War of 1914-18. Afterwards there were second hand engines available, and trained mechanics were being demobbed. Windermere was one of the earliest venues for experimenting, testing and racing motor boats.

By 1923 and 1924 the Ambleside carnivals were including the first races for motor boats. In 1923 there were 34 entries: 7 for the under 10 h.p. race, 8 for over 10 h.p., and 4 hydroplanes. 16 competed in the open race, which included several who had already appeared. The trophies presented then, such as the Waterhead Challenge Rose Bowl and Sir George McKay's Cup, are still being raced for. In 1925 the carnival was at Windermere. As well as motorboat racing it included a race for sailing yachts, decorated cars, motorcycles, bicycles and a gymkhana. A good time was had by all. The last Ambleside Carnival was held in 1931.

Once motor boats had developed to this stage it did not take long for some of those involved to meet and decide to form a motor boat club.

PROGRAMMES 3d. EACH.

AMBLESIDE
WATER CARNIVAL
and FISHING COMPETITION.

WATERHEAD BAY, AMBLESIDE,

SATURDAY, AUGUST 25th, 1923.

President : COL. F. HAWORTH, J.P.   Vice-Pres : G. G. WORDSWORTH, Esq

PATRONS :

Mrs. Bruce, Mrs. Creyke, Mrs. Feirn, Mrs. Gatey, Mrs. Gardham, Misses Leith, Mrs. MacIver, Miss Smalley, Mrs. Warburton, Sir G. Mills McKay, Sir A. Lindsay Parkinson, Geo. Aitchison, Esq., T. B. Atkinson, Esq., W. S. Asplin, Esq., Rev. J. B. Bolland, J. Collier, Esq., A. S. Dixon, Esq., — Dawson, Esq., A. B. Dunlop, Esq., Major R. H. Edmondson, A. J. Freeman, Esq., Geo. Gatey, Esq., N. Gatey, Esq., Geo. Grundy, Esq., G. Gascoigne, Esq., J. H. Hacking, Esq., Col. F. Haworth, O. W. E. Hedley, Esq., ... Esq., W. D Heelis, Esq., A. H. Illingworth, Esq., R. W. F. Jenkinson, Esq., C. Lings, Esq., — Lees, Jun., Esq., ... Mason, Esq., J. M. Sladen, Esq., A. R. Sladen, Esq., T. Scott, Esq., E. A. Todd, Esq., John Taylor, Esq., C.B.E., John Toison, Esq., G. C. Wordsworth, Esq., J. B. Willows, Esq., Major E. F. Wrigley, F. A. Whitwell, Esq., Stanley Waddilove, Esq., Messrs. S. Alcock & Co., Ltd., Redditch, L.M.&S. Railway Co., Ltd., Loughrigg Private Hotel, Lakes Herald, Ltd., Lake District Road Traffic Co., Ltd., Provincial Insurance Co., Ltd., Waterhead Boating Co., Waterhead Hotel & Hydro, Ltd., and Others

PROGRAMME

1-30 p.m.—FISHING.   Rods only.   Not more than 2 rods and 2 competitors per boat. Start from Central Motor Boat Pier at 1-30 p.m.   One gun at 3 p.m.   Two guns at 3-15 p.m.   Return to Central Motor Boat Pier not later than 3-30 p.m.

BOUNDARIES.   From Head of Lake to a line between Green Tuft and Holme Crag, excluding Pull Wyke Bay beyond a line between Seamew Crag and Cross's Pier as per map displayed at Boatlandings. No licensed boatman or member of Committee to compete.   Entries 1s. per boat. Weigher-in—Mr. A. E. Huddlestone.

TWO CLASSES.

PIKE (a) Heaviest Catch. 1st Prize, Illingworth Reel; 2nd Prize Pike Reel. (b) Heaviest Catch by bona fide Visitors.   Prize, Landing Net.

PERCH (a) Heaviest Catch. 1st Prize, value £1 0s 0d., 2nd Prize, value 10s. (b) Heaviest Catch by bona fide Visitors.   Prize, Pannier.

"HERALD" PRINTING WORKS, AMBLESIDE.

LEFT   Ambleside Water Carnival Programme, 1923

RIGHT   A boat of the future, early 1900s (source unknown)

THE ARTS AND THE CRAFTS

THE STUDIO MAGAZINE CHAMPIONED THOSE WHO SAW NO DISTINCTION BETWEEN ART FOR ART'S SAKE AND PRACTICAL CRAFTSMANSHIP.

LEFT   The terrace at Broad Leys, 1911

ABOVE   Portrait of C.F.A. Voysey

CHARLES FRANCIS ANNESLEY VOYSEY (1857-1941).

The Studio, 'An Illustrated Magazine of Fine and Applied Art', made its debut in 1893. Its founder was Charles Holme, who in 1889 had moved into William Morris's own Red House. It set out to bridge the gaps between high art, professional designers, and the cultivated middle class. The cover of the first issue, April 1893, was designed by a relatively young and unknown architect and designer called Charles Voysey.

From the start The Studio, beautifully illustrated in half tone and colour, championed Voysey, Mackintosh, Baillie Scott, Aubrey Beardsley, Walter Crane, and others who saw no distinction between art for art's sake and practical craftsmanship. Voysey's pungent and trenchant articles - he didn't pull any punches and seemed totally certain in his views - made attractive reading. There was nothing parochial about The Studio. It was influential in Europe and America, carrying the names of the British Arts and Crafts Movement far and wide, and in turn brought Continental and American artists and designers to the attention of the British. Today it is called Studio International.

Publications played a big part in the short

but widespread success of the Arts and Crafts Movement. Country Life, founded in 1897 by Edward Hudson (for whom Lutyens built Deanery Garden at Sonning in 1901), was another champion of Voysey, including an article in 1899 on Voysey's own house The Orchard before it was even finished. Voysey himself had been much influenced by a magazine called The Hobby Horse, published by The Century Guild from 1884, which with its beautiful typography and layout was an Arts and Crafts object in itself. Charles Voysey, even before he had built much, was regarded as someone to be looked up to, even revered. He was held up as a man to whom life and art were inseparable, who lived and worked according to the highest principles; a man who could cut through Victorian cant and hypocrisy and design a house free of superfluous frippery.

A man of intense feeling and emotion rigorously held in check. This of course is a subjective impression of Voysey, arrived at more than half a century after his death. It is supported by one of his favourite design motifs, a heart and a crown: 'the heart which is love, crowned with the restraining diadem of self control'. A cover design

VOL. I. NO. 1. APRIL, 1893.

THE STUDIO

AN ILLVSTRATED MAGAZINE OF FINE AND APPLIED ART.

Artists as Craftsmen. No. I.
Sir Frederic Leighton as a Modeller.

The Growth of Recent Art.
By R. A. M. STEVENSON.

A New Illustrator: Aubrey
Beardsley. By JOSEPH PENNELL.

Spitalfields Brocades.
By LASENBY LIBERTY.

Designing for Book-plates.

Spain as a Sketching Ground.
By FRANK BRANGWYN.

The Newlyn Point of View.

The Grafton Gallery.
By C. W. FURSE.

News of the Month. Reviews, &c. &c.

With Auto-lithograph (33 × 15),
"WEED BURNERS IN THE FENS."
By R. W. MACBETH, A.R.A.

SIXPENCE OFFICES: 16 HENRIETTA ST., COVENT GARDEN. LONDON MONTHLY

Annual Subscription, Seven Shillings and Sixpence, Post Free.

'IF YOU HAD WANDERED THROUGH VARIOUS ROOMS OF THE ARTS CLUB IN DOVER STREET, LONDON, AT ANY TIME AFTER ELEVEN O'CLOCK IN THE MORNING UNTIL ABOUT THE SAME TIME AT NIGHT, YOU WOULD ALMOST CERTAINLY HAVE NOTICED AN ELDERLY GENTLEMAN WITH FEATURES GREATLY DISTINGUISHED BY THE CUT OF HIS NOSE AND THE ARCH OF HIS BROW...'
ROBERT DONAT'S AFFECTIONATE TRIBUTE TO HIS UNCLE-IN-LAW

for The Studio depicted male and female figures, she holding the lily of purity (and art), while he holds a planets type governor for the steam engine, representing usefulness and control. Another subjective impression is of a natural bachelor. In fact this is incorrect; he had married Mary Maria Evans in 1885, and they had five children, of whom Charles, Annesley and Priscilla survived early childhood. He built his famous house, The Orchard, for them in 1898-99. Sadly they had to sell in 1906, and the couple separated in 1917. Voysey ended his days - he lived until 1944 - between his small flat in St James's Street and the Arts Club.

He was a small and slight man with pale blue eyes and thinning sandy hair. He designed his own

'REPOSE, CHEERFULNESS, SIMPLICITY, BREADTH, WARMTH, QUIETNESS IN A STORM, ECONOMY OF UPKEEP, EVIDENCE OF PROTECTION, HARMONY WITH SURROUNDINGS, ABSENCE OF DARK PASSAGES, EVEN-NESS OF TEMPERATURE, AND MAKING THE HOUSE A FRAME FOR ITS INMATES. DOORS WIDE ON PROPORTION, TO SUGGEST A WELCOME, NOT STANDOFFISHLY DIGNIFIED LIKE A COFFIN LID. IN THE OFFICES FOR THE SERVANTS TO USE, LET THEM BE CHEERFUL AND NOT SHABBY AND DARK. RICH AND POOR ALIKE APPRECIATE THESE QUALITIES'.

VOYSEY'S OWN RECIPE FOR A GOOD HOUSE

clothing, including the bright blue shirts architects still like to wear, avoiding anything that harboured dirt or dust. He was clean and prim and gentle in his ways, but of firm disposition. Punctual, with businesslike habits; correspondence was dealt with immediately, the hours of work strictly adhered to. His letters to contractors show how much he hated any negligence, but he was equally strict with himself. He designed, drew and managed every detail of his buildings, never employing a site clerk and only allowing pupils (no more than two or three) to make copies. The site survey by Mawson for Moor Crag is the only time he employed someone else to do this. He was meticulous about expenses. Voysey did not take holidays, and disapproved of studying foreign building as so many of his compatriots did. Although his architectural practice withered away after 1909 or so, he was a prolific and eminently successful designer of wallpapers, fabrics and furniture to the end of his life. He was curiously dismissive of his own wallpaper designs, as was William Morris, although he used them in his own house and at Broad Leys.

His architectural drawings are decisive, washed in clear bright colours. There are few preparatory drawings, nor did he use a rubber much.

Christine Leach, granddaughter, told us that when in 1898 Arthur Currer Briggs came to commission a house in Windermere, 'he would have gone to the best'.

RIGHT The main entrance at Broad Leys

G.H. PATTINSON

The Pattinson family are a unifying factor in this book, central to the story of both the house and of the club. George Henry Pattinson (1856-1941), took control of the firm in about the late 1870s. Like his father before him he was ready to seize on an opportunity and eager to learn. Pattinsons were the great Windermere builders, speculators and entrepreneurs at the turn of the century. Their yard was at Elim Grove, on the road out of Bowness towards Windermere.

Voysey's relationship with his builder, George (G.H.) Pattinson, was a prickly one. His letters, now at Kendal Record Office, are short to the point of being peremptory, and we feel rather sorry for Pattinson. However those were the days when 'by return of post' might mean the same day, and we should perhaps understand them as the equivalent of today's e-mails. Voysey was very sharp with Pattinson's occasional shortcomings 'I am not called upon to trust or mistrust you but to act strictly according to the letter of the agreement' (letter Aug 27 1900). However when a mistake was Voysey's own, as with the porthole window at Moor Crag

ABOVE   G.H. Pattinson

PATTINSONS WERE THE GREAT WINDERMERE BUILDERS, SPECULATORS AND ENTREPRENEURS AT THE TURN OF THE CENTURY

LEFT   The Nook (now Overmere), a Pattinson home built in 1895

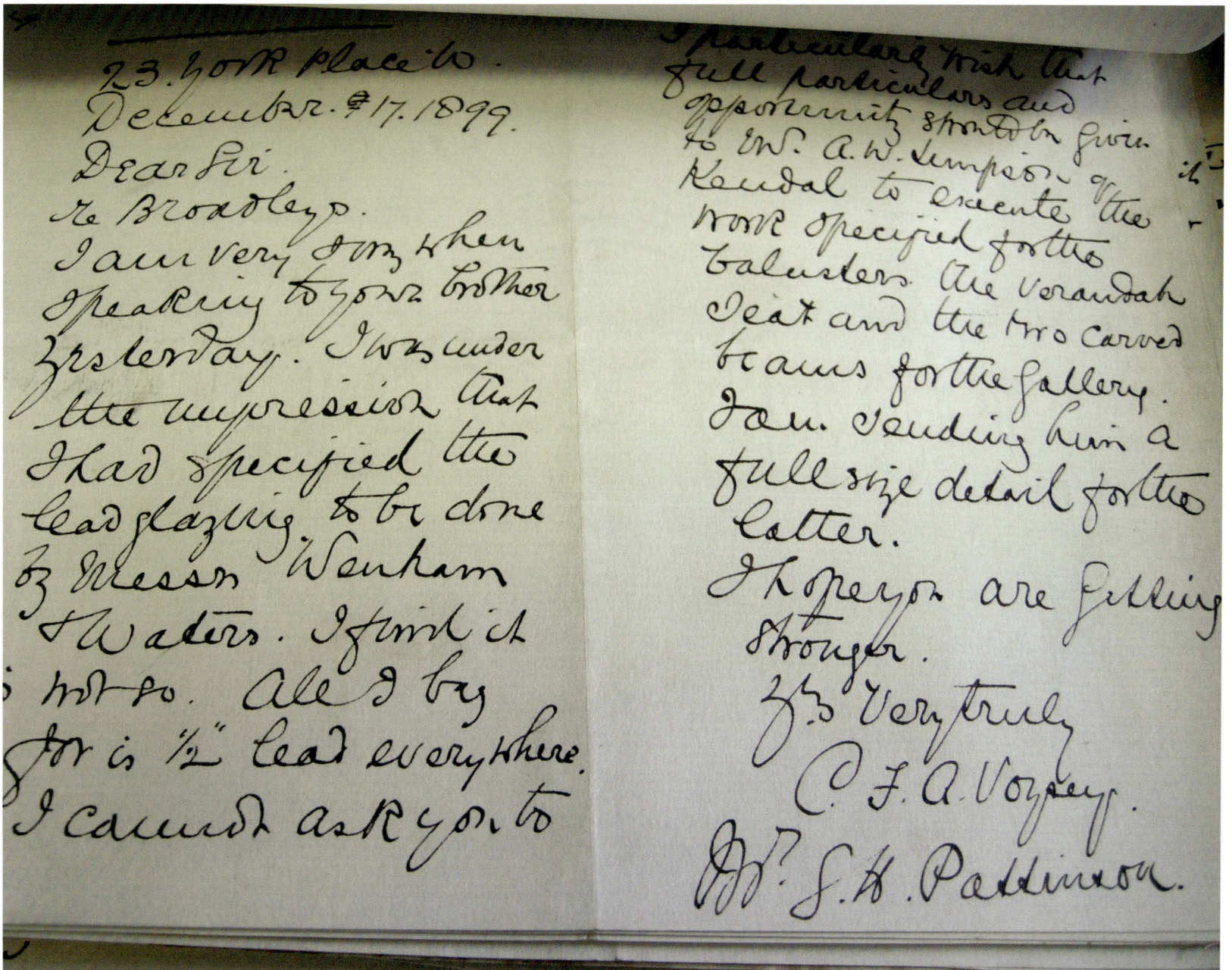

23 York Place W.
December 17. 1899.
Dear Sir,
re Broadleys.
I am very sorry when speaking to your brother yesterday. I was under the impression that I had specified the lead glazing to be done by Messrs Wenham & Waters. I find it is not so. All I beg for is ½" lead everywhere. I cannot ask you to

I particularly wish that full particulars and opportunity should be given to Mr. A. W. Simpson of Kendal to execute the work specified for the balusters. The verandah seat and the two carved beams for the gallery. I am sending him a full size detail for the latter.
I hope you are getting stronger.
Yrs very truly
C. F. A. Voysey.
Mr. G. H. Pattinson.

ABOVE Letter between Voysey and Pattinson regarding the building of Broad Leys.
(With kind permission of Kendal Archive Centre, Kendal Ref: WDB 133/2/85)

(Dec 6 1900) he readily admitted it, and paid for it to be put right.

G.H.'s younger brother Joseph (c.1860) trained as an architect, and naturally designed many of their houses. However they also contracted to build designs by other architects, such as Voysey's two Windermere houses, Broad Leys and Moor Crag. Did Pattinsons learn from building these revolutionary houses? For an answer we have only to look at their other houses before and after. In 1895, for example, G.H. built Overmere (originally The Nook), on Longtail Hill, to a design by his brother Joseph, for F. Coop of Southport. It is thoroughly and typically Victorian. The materials are a real Victorian mix: local green stone laid dry for the base, red rock-faced sandstone for the dressings, and timber-framing above, with big pegs. The plan is conventionally Victorian too - a large square with the staircase conventionally in the middle. Rooms are tall and boxy, with elaborate skirting boards, cornices, moulded doorcases and fireplaces. The stair has spiral turned balusters and an elaborately turned newel post. Everything has a machine finish, and there are lots of surfaces to keep dusted.

Just a dozen years later, in 1907-11, George H. Pattinson built a big house called Gossel Ridding for himself, to demonstrate just what he and the firm could do. The architect was again his brother Joseph, but what a change! Gossel Ridding shines in every department. It is Voysey-like in many respects, white and spreading, with mullioned windows, round chimneys and a big green roof.

The interior woodwork is superb, like Simpson's work but more so. The garden is Mawson like, with balustraded terraces. It tries to outdo all of these gentlemen, forgetting perhaps that you cannot go one better than perfection.

A generation later E.H. (Harold) Pattinson, son of G.H. was joint founder, first commodore, and general stalwart of the Windermere Motor Boat Club. His twin brother Thomas Cooper (1890-1971) succeeded his father as head of the firm.

ABOVE   Fireplace detail from Gossel Ridding
BELOW   Gossel Ridding built by G.H. Pattinson, 1907 -11

ARTHUR SIMPSON OF KENDAL

With Arthur Simpson (1857-1922), a central figure in the Cumbrian Arts and Crafts story, Voysey had a happier relationship. Indeed he became a particular friend and they corresponded regularly.

Simpson provided the decorative woodwork at Broad Leys, at Blackwell, and probably at Moor Crag.

After working with George Faulkner Armitage in Altrincham, in 1883 Simpson took three cottages knocked into one (empty since the Collingwoods left) at Ghyll Head. This was the family home in the summer, with workshop and teaching space.

He also taught at the Keswick School for Industrial Arts 1896, which had been founded by Hardwicke Rawnsley and his wife Edith after frequent visits to Ghyll Head.

In 1901 he moved his home and showroom to The Handicrafts, Church Street, Windermere. Simpson's furniture is still much prized today.

TOP   Littleholme, Kendal. Built for Arthur Simpson by Voysey in 1909

ABOVE   Arthur Simpson

ANNIE GARNETT (1864-1942)

The Garnett family lived at Fairfield in Bowness, a cute dolls' house (the family called it that) built by Pattinson in the 1860s. Just below it was the Crown Hotel, now Crown Rigg, which was the family business. Curiously, Fairfield has just one unmistakable Voysey fireplace, of pale blue vertical tiles laid in a shallow U, with a segmental hearth with pullout drawer underneath. This fireplace is provocatively placed under a window (provoking the questions - where does the smoke go?), in a small sitting room which is mostly window. Stimulated by a visit to the Langdale linen industry at Elterwater, Annie set up an Arts and Crafts enterprise called The Spinnery in 1891, using the stable and coach house that fronts her home. In 1912 she expanded down the hill into the New Spinnery, incorporating showroom and teaching space. It is now a restaurant. However the industry did not long survive the First World War.

Annie was a close friend of Helen Currer Briggs, who furnished Broad Leys with light embroidered fabrics, many of which must be from the Spinnery. She was an honoured guest of the Mayor and

STIMULATED BY A VISIT TO THE LANGDALE LINEN INDUSTRY AT ELTERWATER, ANNIE SET UP AN ARTS AND CRAFTS ENTERPRISE CALLED THE SPINNERY IN 1891

LEFT   Annie Garnett with sister Frances

RIGHT   Voysey fireplace at Fairfield

Mayoress at Gledhow Grange for the big Leeds Triennial Music Festival, as was Charles Voysey. 'Mr Briggs told us he has got tickets for me for the whole festival if I would have it and Mrs Briggs insisted on my staying over with them, I could not resist it. I love music so.' Gledhow Grange was in North Leeds, 3 miles from the centre 'quite a rush each day getting in and out'. Christine Leach remembered being taken from Pull Wyke to see 'Barnie Garnett' (Annie's sister Frances, who outlived her) in '...the house up the hill out of Bowness, seeing her sitting in her sitting room near an open window with red squirrels outside. Lots of linen around.'

THOMAS MAWSON

Voysey himself designed the framework for a garden for Broad Leys, indicating the terrace in front of the house and the sunken garden at the side. Beyond that there is a network of rough paved paths dropping down between shrubs and small trees to the lake shore, but leaving a large area free for the daffodils that, as Annie Garnett tells us, were there before the house. So Voysey's outline was clearly developed by someone else.

Was it Mawson? A central figure in the Arts and Crafts movement, not least by the title of his own book The Arts and Crafts of Garden Making (1st edition 1900), he is the most likely candidate - although there is no record to confirm this.

Thomas Mawson (1861-1933) was a Lancastrian who, with his two brothers, set up a nursery garden and landscape design enterprise in Windermere. Thomas being the landscape designer. His first job was across the lake at Bryerswood, a new house built for Joseph Ridgeway Bridson. The house has gone but the garden remains. The architect, R. Knill Freeman, was also working for Colonel Sandys at Graythwaite Hall. This led to Mawson's first really big contract, and in turn to a partnership with the young architect Dan Gibson. Together they built and landscaped, from a virgin site, Brockhole near Troutbeck. That was in 1897-1902, so it is exactly contemporary with Broad Leys, Moor Crag and Blackwell. It was an astonishing time!

It is not an obvious Mawson garden however, as a visit to his gardens at Langdale Chase or Brockhole will confirm. No balustrading, no pergola (or was there one by the croquet lawn?), not enough terracing or formal Italianate steps. Rupert Potter's photographs, taken only a dozen years later, show a densely planted and very lush garden. Today it is considerably simplified.

LEFT Fairfield, home of Annie Garnett in Bowness-on-Windermere

ABOVE Thomas Mawson

BELOW Brockhole in Windermere with its Mawson designed garden

ARTHUR CURRER BRIGGS OF BROAD LEYS

'A TRUE VICTORIAN GENTLEMAN'

CHRISTINE LEACH, GRANDDAUGHTER

LEFT In the garden at Broad Leys

BELOW From left to right Arthur b.1855, Gerald b.1860, Gilbert
(Bertie) b.1863 & Ernest Currer Briggs b.1866, taken
arround 1880

The eldest son of Henry Briggs and Catherine
Shepherd, he was born in 1855 at Outwood Hall
near Wakefield. There were five children: Arthur,
Marion, Gerald, Gilbert (Bertie) and Ernest.

In 1883 Arthur married Helen Jones and they
made their home in Leeds. They had three children:

Dorothy (Dodie), Reginald, and Donald.

Annie Garnett in her journal has left us a charming
portrait: 'He is a very delightful person at once
clever in an intelligent kind of way and very modest,
knows things thoroughly not just on the surface,
what he knows he knows of his own knowledge.'

Arthur and Helen had been visiting the Lake District for several years before they commissioned Broad Leys. They owned Pull Wyke at the north end of Windermere, where Arthur's brother Ernest lived for a time. Bertie (Gilbert) lived near the golf course in a substantial house called The Oaks.

Arthur's mother Catherine ('Gran' in the letters) lived a short distance from Broad Leys in the fine boathouse built for Ghyll Head. An early interest in the Arts and Crafts is shown by Helen and Ernest, who are listed as guarantors for the Kendal Arts, Crafts and Loan exhibition in 1891.

'TO US BOYS HE HE WAS A GOOD READER OF BOOKS LIKE THE JUNGLE BOOK OR KING SOLOMON'S MINES WHEN HE CAME HOME TIRED IN THE EVENING AND WANTED A BIT OF PEACE, SO WE SAT ON THE ARMS OF HIS ARMCHAIR AND LISTENED'.

DONALD BRIGGS IN HIS MEMOIR OF 1971 *THE RECORD OF A YORKSHIRE FAMILY* RECALLING SOMETHING OF HIS FATHER'S CHARACTER.

ABOVE Arthur and Helen in the early days of their marriage

LEFT Sketch of Arthur by his brother Ernest *(with kind permission from Leeds University Library, Special Collections, K.M. Briggs Collection. MS 1309)*

'HE WAS A VERY TIDY PERSON, PARTICULARLY WITH FISHING TACKLE'.
DONALD BRIGGS

THE INDUSTRIALIST

The family business was coal. Henry Briggs Son & Co owned and ran a major coal mining enterprise at Whitwood, near Wakefield, in the West Yorkshire coalfield. It was a family affair; all the brothers were on the board, though Ernest, who was said to be 'useless in the pits' (Elizabeth Buchanan) became a watercolourist. Ernest's daughter Katherine Briggs was an important folklore expert and author. Her papers are collected at Leeds University.

Arthur unexpectedly had to take charge of Henry Briggs Son & Co Ltd when he was only 26, following the sudden and unexpected death in 1881 of his father Henry in Norway while he was visiting Bratsberg silver mines. It was a huge responsibility

for someone so young. The colliery was a massive undertaking, employing at its peak more than six thousand people and producing a million and more tons of coal a year. It was moreover a complete source to sale operation: coal was transported on the company's rails from mine to canal, then down the Aire & Calder navigation in their 'Tom Pudding' compartment boats to the inland port of Goole. From there four company steamships traded to Europe.

Under Arthur's direction the company expanded and diversified its markets still further. Small coal and slack for instance was a perennial nuisance, virtually a waste product. So in 1883 he formed

ABOVE Henry Briggs Son & Co coal mining enterprise at Whitwood, West Yorkshire

BELOW Letterhead of Arthur Currer Briggs

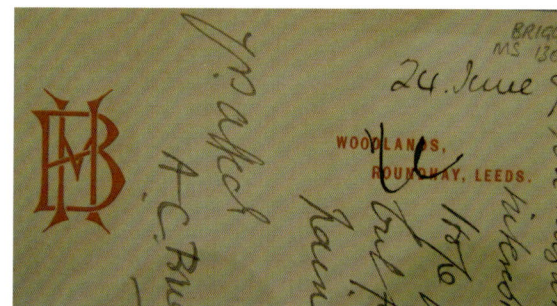

'HE ALWAYS SEEMED OF VERY EVEN TEMPER, AND NEVER INCLINED TO REBUKE EVEN IF WELL DESERVED.'

DONALD BRIGGS

a joint company with Demster & Co of Elland to manufacture coke, gas, benzol and sulphate of ammonia. Noisome products it is true - it is easy to see why an escape to the pure air and limpid waters of the Lake District was such an attraction - but the Whitwood Chemical Company Limited was a highly successful venture. Benzol was exported to Germany for the manufacture of the synthetic dyes the Victorians loved so much, such as mauve and magenta. Coke went to Scandinavia and the gas was used to light the district.

Bricks were needed for building so the company made its own. Bricks stamped HBW are often found in the area.

In 1897 Arthur proposed the foundation of a Coal Owners' Association. This did not come to fruition, but a West Yorkshire Coal Owners' Association was formed.

The family's ties with Whitwood were finally severed when industry was nationalised in 1947 and Whitwood colliery itself was wound up and closed in about 1970. Reginald Briggs had joined the board in 1917, followed by his brother Donald in 1919. It was a difficult time, as confrontations between labour and management culminated in the general strike in 1926. 'It has by chance been my lot to dismantle the important commercial ventures which owed their beginning and success to the work, energy and foresight of my Great Grandfather, my Grandfather and my Father..' Donald Briggs remembered in 1971.

BELOW Henry Briggs Son & Co coal mining enterprise at Whitwood, West Yorkshire

HOVSES·FOR·MESSRS·HY·BRIGGS·&·SON·
AT·WHITWOOD·NORMATON·YORKSHIRE·
C·F·A·VOYSEY·ARCHITECT·23·YORK·PLACE·W·
Invtet delt.

THE PHILANTHROPIST.

Henry Briggs Son & Co was regarded as a progressive and enlightened company. In 1863 the concept of profit sharing and co-operative management was introduced by Henry Briggs. This served to bring to end a thirteen week strike, i.e. it was a practical solution to a problem as much as philanthropy. Profit sharing was conditional on there being no further strikes, and that all disputes had to be settled by arbitration. The success of the scheme is shown by the fact that more than 300 miners bought company shares and two employees at a time were elected to the board.

In 1904 Arthur Currer Briggs commissioned

ABOVE Voysey's Whitwood design for Arthur Currer Briggs 1904/5. The right-hand range was not built.

C.F.A. Voysey, the architect of his Lake District house, to build miners' cottages and an institute at Whitwood. The first design of 1904 came out too expensive at £12,950, A reduced design, with ten fewer houses, was made in 1905. They were built in 1906-8 by Joseph Pullan & Sons of Leeds at the cost of £8,028.

The nineteen houses of Whitwood Terrace lie back from the high road behind square front gardens and privet hedges. Gabled houses alternate with pairs of dormered and slightly smaller houses, which gives a pleasing rhythm. Big square roughcast chimneys dominate the composition, with the tapered and slightly bellied pots that have been replaced at Broad Leys, for safety. Big rosemary tiled roofs, wooden gutters on typical Voysey curled brackets, white roughcast. Inside, the clever use of space

ABOVE   Whitwood today, showing the Institute (now Rising Sun Inn) and the tower of the manager's house

enabled him to provide each house with two good living rooms, four bedrooms and a bathroom. In 1908 this was very advanced for working class housing.

Repose, cheerfulness, simplicity, breadth, warmth, quietness in a storm, economy of upkeep, evidence of protection, harmony with surroundings, absence of dark passages, even-ness of temperature, and making the house a frame for its inmates. All the Voysey qualities are there, in miniature.

At the end of the terrace is a bigger building with a tower: the Institute, generally called the 'Stute. It is now the Rising Sun Inn. Although it was clearly intended as an alternative to the pub, it never was teetotal. Although staunchly nonconformist neither Arthur nor Helen were puritan in outlook - indeed Helen 'liked her whisky' - and nor was Voysey. The idea was to make social drinking more civilised. Voysey's experience here stood him in good stead later, when in 1916 he joined the State Management Scheme that was brought in for pubs and breweries in and around Carlisle and Gretna

to cope with the massive influx of armaments workers.

The Institute is long, low and comfortable-looking with a verandah in front: old English hospitality personified. Inside there are good fireplaces and some stained glass, but Voysey's specially designed furniture has gone. The main rooms have vertical boarding with a fillet to dado level, as at Moor Crag, and a little bracketed plate rack, but they are of stained pine not oak.

On the corner plot, and setting off the whole composition, is the white tower of the manager's house. Voysey liked to design an occasional tower to contrast with the insistent horizontality of most of his buildings. This one is of four storeys, with a low pyramid roof which originally sported a weathervane in the shape of one of the beetles that infested the site - a typical touch of humour. The interesting fenestration indicates the staircase and the main rooms within. It has good interior detail reminiscent of Broad Leys, with hugely wide fireplaces and plank doors with typical latches and

'HE IS A VERY DELIGHTFUL PERSON AT ONCE CLEVER IN AN INTELLIGENT KIND OF WAY AND VERY MODEST, KNOWS THINGS THOROUGHLY NOT JUST ON THE SURFACE, WHAT HE KNOWS HE KNOWS OF HIS OWN KNOWLEDGE.'

ANNIE GARNETT

REPOSE, CHEERFULNESS, SIMPLICITY, BREADTH, WARMTH, QUIETNESS IN A STORM, ECONOMY OF UPKEEP, EVIDENCE OF PROTECTION, HARMONY WITH SURROUNDINGS.

long strap hinges. The closely slatted staircase too is typical, the newels going right up to the ceiling and horizontal (and not very useful) handrails.

The whole ensemble of cottages, Institute and tower is undeniably attractive, but that is not the primary aim. Like the profit sharing scheme this is practical philanthropy, rather than the deliberate creation of a showpiece like Lord Leverhulme's Port Sunlight.

Directly opposite the Institute, across the lane, is a large nondescript industrial estate of anonymous sheds. Here was until 1970 the huge Whitwood Colliery with its winding wheels, its railway sidings and shrieking engines and clanging wagons, its dirt and its smell. Trams rattled along the main road to an octagonal tram shelter at the junction. Tramping miners passed by in their hundreds at shift change time. It is hard to imagine today.

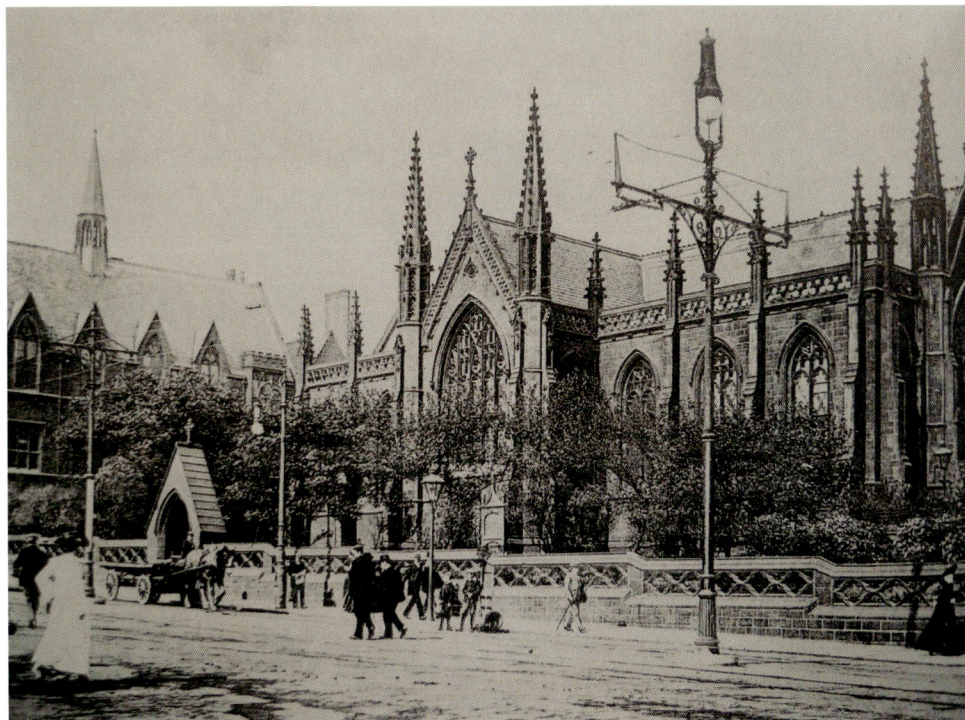

RIGHT   Mill Hill Chapel, Leeds

BELOW   The memorial to Arthur Currer Briggs at Whitwood

IN MEMORY OF
ARTHUR CURRER BRIGGS
BORN 1855.   DIED 1906.

THE NONCONFORMIST

Nineteenth century industrial entrepreneurs were very often dissenters in their religious observance. Grandfather Henry Briggs had been a Unitarian lay preacher at Wakefield's Westgate Chapel, a large and dignified Georgian building of 1752 by the station car park. His son Henry was another strict Unitarian, and Arthur followed suit. It was rational Christianity; it made more sense to the businesslike mind than the traditional Trinitarian church.

In Arthur's time the family had switched their

allegiance to the Mill Hill Chapel in Leeds. Rebuilt in 1848 by J.S. Crowther it was, with Gee Cross Chapel at Hyde, the first nonconformist chapel in the country to be fully gothic, like a parish church: a major bid for respectability. In fact it echoes the design of the recently completed Leeds Parish Church, but is more scholarly and correct in its gothic detail. An uptight building, little loved today, providing an interesting contrast to the free and almost style less elegance of Voysey's work at Windermere and Whitwood.

THE LORD MAYOR.

Arthur Currer Briggs was Mayor of Leeds in 1903-4. He was elected in odd circumstances. When the selected mayor was technically ruled out of taking office, he was elected mayor despite having had no previous political career. Despite the inauspicious start it turned out to be an exceptionally successful mayoralty.

'His appointment to the Civic Chair was a double revelation: it revealed a man of business aptitude hitherto unknown to public life, and it revealed a lady, who by her fascinating oratory, and her overwhelming duty to the cause of charity in many forms was a distinguished acquisition to the life of the city'. Helen's story is expanded elsewhere.

1903-4 was a good year for Leeds, when a number of big schemes reached their fruition. The University of Leeds was inaugurated with great ceremony. A Trades Union Congress gathered in the city. The Triennial Music Festival, in which the Currer Briggs took great interest, took place. They invited both Annie Garnett and Charles Voysey to join them for the festival. The famous Kirkgate Market opened, one of the largest and finest covered markets in Europe. Two hospitals were opened as well.

VERY FEW MEN INDEED HAVE SET SO NOBLE AN EXAMPLE, WHETHER IN PUBLIC OR PRIVATE LIFE AND CONSEQUENTLY VERY FEW HAVE HAD SO GREAT AN INFLUENCE FOR GOOD.

DONALD BRIGGS
THE RECORD OF A YORKSHIRE FAMILY

LEFT   Arthur Currer Briggs as Lord Mayor of Leeds, 1903/04

THE MOTORIST.

Arthur Currer Briggs was an early enthusiast for a new mode of transport, the motor car. His is the first name in the Leeds register, and the numberplate U1 is still reserved for the Mayor of Leeds. His first car was a 10hp Lanchester: the first Lanchesters were marketed in 1901. Arthur's own Motor Register Book is preserved, containing a record of his journeys from June 1904 to his death in 1906. The book itself, curiously, is an Arts & Crafts object, silk-covered. In it he records a typical journey of 5 1/2 hrs from Leeds to Broad Leys with 40 minutes for lunch. He motored for pleasure round the Lakes as well. In 1919 Helen Currer Briggs registered a car too.

ABOVE Arthur, Helen and other family members in their car outside Broad Leys

AND ELECTRICITY.

Interestingly for the head of a coal company producing coal gas, Arthur Currer Briggs was a pioneering enthusiast for electricity. He promoted electrical development to reduce smoke pollution and nuisance in Leeds, being a founder member of the Yorkshire Electric Power Company. Electric lighting for houses had been introduced for the first time in 1880 at Cragside, in Northumberland. Broad Leys was electrically lit from a mains supply from the start. Moor Crag has a 12v system and special clip-on 'Moor Crag' lights instead.

It is interesting that the Arts and Crafts houses of Windermere, which hark back to an age of traditional craftsmanship and simplicity, depended for their existence on the newly forged railway system and the even more recent motor car, and for their pleasant ambience - and low ceilings - on the even newer fangled introduction of electricity.

THIS·HOUSE
WAS·BVILT·B
Y·ARTHVR·CVR
RER·BRIGGS
&·HELEN·HIS
WIFE·IN·1899

DESIGNED·BY·C·F·A·VOYSEY·

THE BUILDING OF BROAD LEYS

THIS • HOVSE
WAS • BVILT • BY
ARTHVR • CVR=
RER • BRIGGS
& • HELEN • HIS
WIFE • IN • 1899

DESIGNED • BY • C.F.A • VOYSEY

LEFT   The stone inscription outside Broad Leys
designed by Voysey

RIGHT   View of Broad Leys from the garden, 1909

So runs the inscription by the front door. The acknowledgment of Voysey as architect, as well as to Arthur and Helen Currer Briggs as clients, is historically unusual, but eminently characteristic of the time. The Arts and Crafts Movement liked to credit the makers and doers. Typical of Voysey himself was the idiosyncratic lettering, and his brusque note of October 17th 1899: 'Kindly instruct the carver that he is on no account to improve on my drawing.....' Voysey insisted on everything, down to the smallest detail, being exactly right.

Thanks to Voysey's letters to his builder, to drawings preserved in London by the RIBA, and to records kept at the house, we can follow the design and construction of Broad Leys and Moor Crag in considerable detail. The two houses were built in tandem, by the same contractors, although Voysey was scrupulous in keeping the two sets of accounts separate. Moor Crag however - referred to by the Ulverston Rural District Council inspector as 'Mr Buckley's cottage' - was always somewhat in arrears.

JAN 7 1899 TENDERS
WERE INVITED:
'GENTLEMEN
I AM INSTRUCTED
BY A. CURRER
BRIGGS ESQR OF
WOODLANDS
ROUNDHAY LEEDS
TO INVITE YOU TO
TENDER FOR THE
WORKS AS SET FORTH
IN THE DRAWINGS
NOS 1 TO 22.'

RIGHT   Presentation perspective
of Broad Leys for Arthur
Currer Briggs.

LEYS · WINDERMERE
Æ · CVRRER · BRIGGS · ESQ

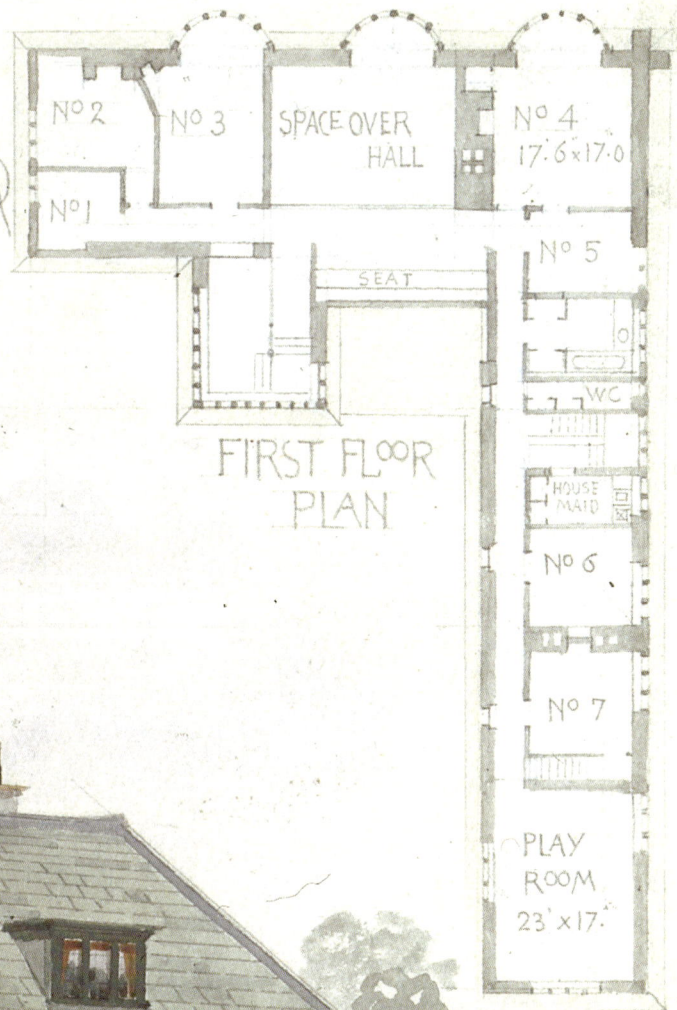

FIRST FLOOR
PLAN

No 2   No 3   SPACE OVER   No 4
                HALL   17·6 x 17·0

No 1

                SEAT   No 5

                              WC

                              HOUSE
                              MAID

                              No 6

                              No 7

                              PLAY
                              ROOM
                              23' x 17'

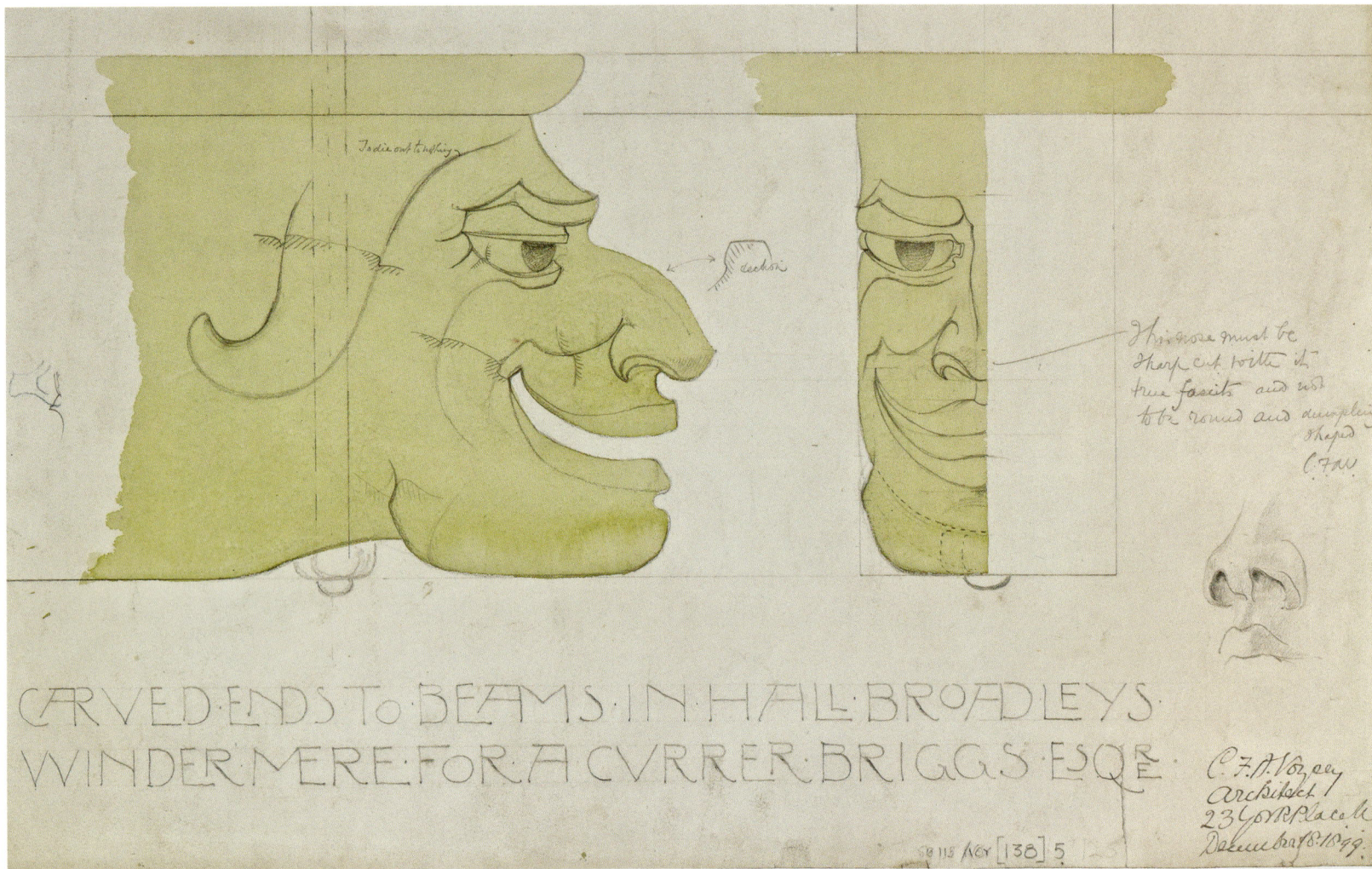

CARVED ENDS TO BEAMS IN HALL BROADLEYS
WINDERMERE FOR A CURRER BRIGGS ESQ.

C.F.A.Voysey
Architect
23 York Place W
December 8 1899.

ABOVE Voysey's original gargoyle detail sketch and
RIGHT   the final carved piece

Voysey's first site visit was on the 8th & 9th May 1898.

June 1898. A drawing (RIBA) shows a proposed house for A. Currer Briggs at Windermere. It has no name yet. L-shaped plan but with only two bows facing the lake. The third bow faces south, lighting the hall with billiard table and gallery - a more complex space than the final version.

On the 18th and 19th June Voysey met Arthur and Helen Currer Briggs in Leeds, presumably to discuss this plan.

By July the essence of the present design was agreed. On 30th August 1898, and only then, the site was bought by Arthur Currer Briggs from Benjamin Townson and George Henry Pattinson for £1,200.

Meanwhile, the design for Moor Crag was causing some problems. A drawing of July 1898 shows an L-shaped house with a servants' wing. Later that month it had been redesigned to a rectangular footprint as now, but with a rectangular bay in the middle and an unsatisfactory internal plan.

In October H. Gaye made the well-known presentation perspective of Broad Leys. All other drawings are by Voysey himself.

On Jan 7 1899 tenders were invited:

'Gentlemen

I am instructed by A. Currer Briggs Esqr of Woodlands Roundhay Leeds to invite you to tender

for the works as set forth in the drawings Nos 1 to 22 inclusive and the specification and memorandum of agreement sent to to you by parcel post today.'

Jan 27 1899. re Broad Leys. I hope you will very soon be prepared to send me your tender for the above. Mr Briggs is very anxious to get on with the work and I am also anxious to get the building roofed in before the summer.

Jan 31 1899. re Broad Leys. I quite approve of the steel joists for openings over 6ft and suppose that by 'wood under' you mean a plate for fixing linings.

26 Feb 1899. Drawing (RIBA) of Broad Leys Lodge as built. The main walling to be the local stone with green slate roofing. Contract price £458. (An earlier design showed attached stables making a U shape round a small yard, which would have been very attractive).

March 27 1899. I am instructed by Mr A Currer Briggs to accept your estimate on March the 6th of four hundred and fifty eight pounds for the lodge. And request you to proceed with the work with all possible speed.

ND but c. May 1899. Leeds Fireclay Company Limited, 20 Park Row to A. Currer Briggs. The bath will leave on Wednesday without fail. The closets were sent last week and should be in Windermere ere this.

June 5 1899. I have arranged to be with Mr Buckley on the 24th in the morning at his ground beyond Broad Leys and should be glad if your foreman could meet me for an inspection of the work at Broad Leys in the afternoon.

June 6 1899. re Broad Leys. I prefer Dorman Long's joists because they are English iron & you will find

ABOVE Small 'porthole' window in Broad Leys' hall

the sizes sharp, marked on stock sizes. The R.S. joist over the drawing room is figured 9 X 5.

June 23 1899. Drawing (Victoria and Albert Museum). House to be built at Cartmel Fell Ghyll Head by Windermere for J.W. Buckley Esquire. Two elevations, two plans. With a note 'This is the plan shown to Mr Buckley at Riggs Hotel Windermere on June 23rd 1899 and approved by him and Mrs Buckley in the presence of Mr Mawson.

There is a similar set for Broad Leys, also at the Victoria and Albert Museum.

Aug 8 1899. Kindly attend to the enclosed (from Ulverston Rural District council). I understood (I think from you) that there were no local authorities to bother us.

Aug 15 1899. Kindly let me know how far on with the lodge you are and when you expect it to be ready for occupation.

Oct 17 1899. Herewith my drawing for the inscription to go on the stone (Broad Leys). Kindly instruct the carver that he is on no account to improve on my drawing. ..to be cut with a V-shaped groove. ..see the stone before it is fixed.

Oct 18 1899. Herewith set of drawings & copy of specification for Mr Buckley's proposed house. Messrs Wenham & Waters contracting for hot and cold water supplies & WCs.

Dec 22 1899. The carved heads are designed and the working drawing is sent to Mr Simpson. (The drawing dated 18 Dec 1899 is in the RIBA collection).

May 9 1900. ...2 coats of paint only, 2 more when Mr Briggs leaves in autumn. (He moved in on the 20 May, in before the house was signed off, and wanted the house free of the smell of paint.)

July 8 1900. I am sorely tempted to keep back your certificate with a view to bringing pressure on Mr Edmondson. He must of course not neglect Broad Leys. As he cannot be in two places at once, if he has undertaken the work for Moor Crag, he ought to be made to send other men at once to get on with the latter. I think the progress is anything but satisfactory. I hope I shall not be forced to a merciless administration of justice.

Sep 13 1900. Broad Leys. I propose to pay my final visit of inspection on the 5th October next. I hope everything will be finished..... certify completion and settle accounts.

Nov 10 1900. I hope to arrive at Windermere on Tuesday next the 13th at 5.5 pm and put up at

BELOW Bedroom at Broad Leys with bow window overlooking the lake

Riggs. Pattinson to come and meet and go through accounts and settle that business before dinner. Mr. Buckley will come at 6.53 from Manchester and they will go to Moor Crag early in the morning meet Messrs Middleton and Townsend at 10 settle electric wiring and other matters. Then settle tradesmans' entrance at Broad Leys & back on the 4.20.

Dec 6 1900. I find you have given Mrs Briggs a very inferior article and cannot justify your payment (housemaid's sink).

24 Jan 1901. Re Moorcrag.
I do not think the above is getting on as well as it ought to be.

July 5 1901. Final account for Moor Crag.

LEFT Stairwell at Broad Leys with original light fitting

ABOVE Voysey designed ventilation grille

THE SPECIFICATIONS

The typescript, dated 6 January 1899, is still at Broad Leys. Here are a few extracts and comments:

House for A. Currer Briggs, to be known as Broad Leys (often written as one word Broadleys at this stage).

- Glazed tiles from Martin Van Straaten.
- Chimney pots from Stanley Bros. Nuneaton. (This was changed. 'Messrs Mitchell of Guildford have made the pots for me and I have found them very satisfactory.' The chimneypots, which were gently bellied from 6" or 7" at the top to 10" at the bottom, were sadly, but necessarily, replaced by plain pipes in 1987-8.)

- Fireplace tiles and grates from Teale Fireplace Co, Leeds.
- Roofing second quality green Westmorland slate from Tilberthwaite. (Voysey preferred second quality because they were less even in tone.) Diminishing courses, copper nails. Laid over 3/4" deal boarding laid diagonally, and felt. The ridges of Hutton Roof stone.
- Ground and first floor up to backstairs all in Austrian oak. All joinery by Messrs Marsh, Jones, Cribb and Co of Lancaster. (The joinery contract went instead to Mr John Edmondson of Biskey Howe Road, Windermere, who judging by Voysey's letters proved less than satisfactory.)

LEFT   Bathroom at Broad Leys with original porcelain bath and hand glazed tiles

BELOW   Entrance door to Broad Leys

- Wrought Iron hinges 15/6 and latches 9/- supplied by W.B. Reynolds of 28 Victoria Street.
- Brass Voysey doorknobs by Messrs Elsley & Co of 30 Great Titchfield Street. 4/- per pair.
- By A.W. Simpson of Kendal: Verandah seats of deal, Stair ballusters with lead inlay 2/4 each, 2 carved heads to gallery cantilevers 10/-.
- 2 best WCs and servants WC.
- Windows: Messrs Wenham & Waters no. 2 Croydon casements with wrought iron long stay fasteners.

- Baths of porcelain supplied by Mr Currer Briggs and carried from Windermere station.
- Wenham & Waters contractors for hot and cold water supplies and WCs. Hot water to be so arranged so that hot water can immediately be drawn off at any one of the hot water taps.
- Two Swinton patent kitchen ranges.
- Windows doorways strings pier caps and stone dressings of best Prudham stone neatly dragged on all faces. (Prudham quarry is near Hexham.)

BROAD LEYS AND MOOR CRAG,
WHILE EACH UNMISTAKABLY
BEARING THE VOYSEY STAMP, ARE
VERY DIFFERENT IN CHARACTER AND
DETAIL.

ABOVE   Oak staircase showing typical heart motif

RIGHT   Full height bay window in the hall at Broad Leys,
with views over the lake

AN EYEWITNESS.

We are lucky to have a first-hand description of the nearly-finished house. It was written by Annie Garnett, whose diary is in Kendal at the Museum of Lakeland Life and Industry.

'Fridy Sep 7 1900. I called on Mrs Currer-Briggs at her new house which Voysey has built; it is delightful; both placing, colouring and style but it is not nearly finished yet; the views are glorious not too extensive... but quite as much as you can enjoy at once and just sufficient to make you appreciate the very spot chosen for the site: it is right on the daffodil mound where we have gathered great bunches of yellow year after year. The grandest feature of the house to my mind is the great hall, just such a one as our ancestors would have built: very simply planned, indeed, I think simplicity one of Voysey's greatest characteristics, there is a great bay window opposite the door you enter from the porch, on the right is an open fire place and a door leading to the dining room. On the left is a door leading to the drawing room and by it the staircase leading up to a long corridor supported by pillars of solid oak. The corridor leads to the two wings of the house where the bedrooms are. The doors are apparently solid oak with no mouldings and quaint conveniently shaped handles. No nails are hidden anywhere: if a nail is a necessity why should it hide its head?

THE GRANDEST FEATURE OF THE HOUSE TO MY MIND IS THE GREAT HALL, JUST SUCH A ONE AS OUR ANCESTORS WOULD HAVE BUILT

BELOW The hall at Broad Leys with impressive full height window showing views of Windermere

RIGHT Part of Annie Garnett's original diary as displayed in Kendal, describing her visit to Broad Leys. *(Courtesy of Abbot Hall, Kendal)*

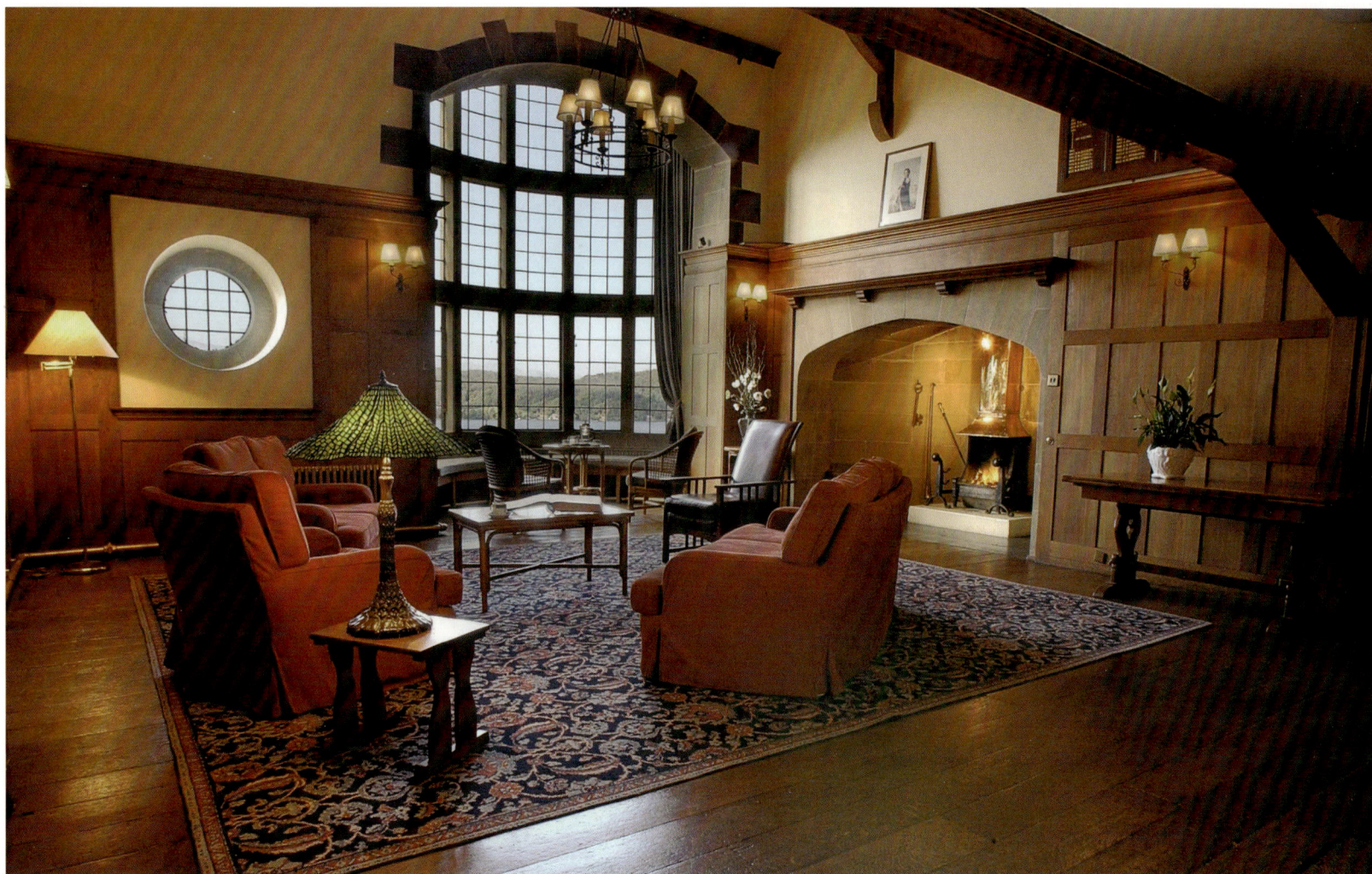

1910

Same anxiety; I sent all the price off yesterday, Sept: 8th 1910

Frid: Sept 7 —   I called on Mr. A Currer-Briggs at her new house which Voysey has built; it is delightful, both placing colouring and style but is not nearly finished yet; the view are glorious not too extensive as from the Lays new house but quite as much as you can enjoy at once and just sufficient to make you appreciate the very spot chosen for the site; it is right on the daffodil mound where we have gathered great bunches of yellow year after year. The grandest feature of the house being used in the great hall, just such a one as our ancestors would have built; very simply planned, indeed I think Simplicity one of Voyseys grandest characteristics, there is a great bay window opposite the door you enter from the porch, on the right is an open fire place and a door leading to the dining room &c; on the left is a door leading to the drawing room and right the staircase leading up to a long corridor supported ~~from the~~ over one end of the hall by pillars of solid oak; the corridor leads to the 2 wings of the house where the bedrooms are. The doors are apparently solid oak with no mouldings and quaint curiously shaped

ABOVE One of the bedroom tiled fireplaces at Broad Leys

Broad Leys and Moor Crag, while each unmistakably bearing the Voysey stamp, are very different in character and detail. Broad Leys is given an air of grandeur by its three bow windows that is completely lacking in Moor Crag, whose great roof and horizontal lines make it look so rooted in the landscape. Voysey evidently saw each job as a separate creation.

Two Arts and Crafts houses by such a fine architect, so close together, are a cause for celebration, but had things turned out differently there could have been two more. In 1898 Voysey made a design for Mr Rickards, near Windermere, to be named Broome Cottage, like a longer and somewhat more elaborate Moor Crag. The Studio was enthusiastic, imagining (Vol 16 1899) 'how this design, with its mingling and modest assertion, would appear to be part of its surroundings'. In 1903 he designed a house on the Rayrigg estate, north of Bowness, for Mr Toulmin MP. This would have resembled Broad Leys, with three curved bows, but with an octagonal lobby to the front door in the angle between the two wings. Although the designs were worked up to the perspective stage, neither was built.

THE LODGE

The lodge provides an interesting foil to the house. In contrast to the white roughcast generally used by Voysey, the local stone is exposed. He did the same at Littleholme in Kendal (1909), for Arthur Simpson. The lodge is a neat pleasing little house, with sloping buttresses, big square chimneys (the far end one has been cut short) and at least one of the original bellied chimneypots.

The plan is clever, without seeming so. The long rectangular footprint has a corner cut out to make a covered porch (as the former verandah of the main house, now filled in). The far end is cross-roofed. The interior is surprising because the floor levels of the cross-roofed part are staggered, with half-flights of stairs up or down from the rest of the house. All the lost spaces under and over stairs are used, nothing is wasted.

In fact both the main house and the lodge use the declivities of the ground to vary the floor levels. In the house the end section of the long service wing nearest the road also has a different set of floor levels, with steps up and down. The difference being that it is all fitted in under one long continuous roof.

Like the main house, the lodge went through several design stages. The first very attractive proposal (Dec 1898) was for a U-shaped block incorporating lodge,

BELOW Voysey's original drawing of the proposed stables and lodge

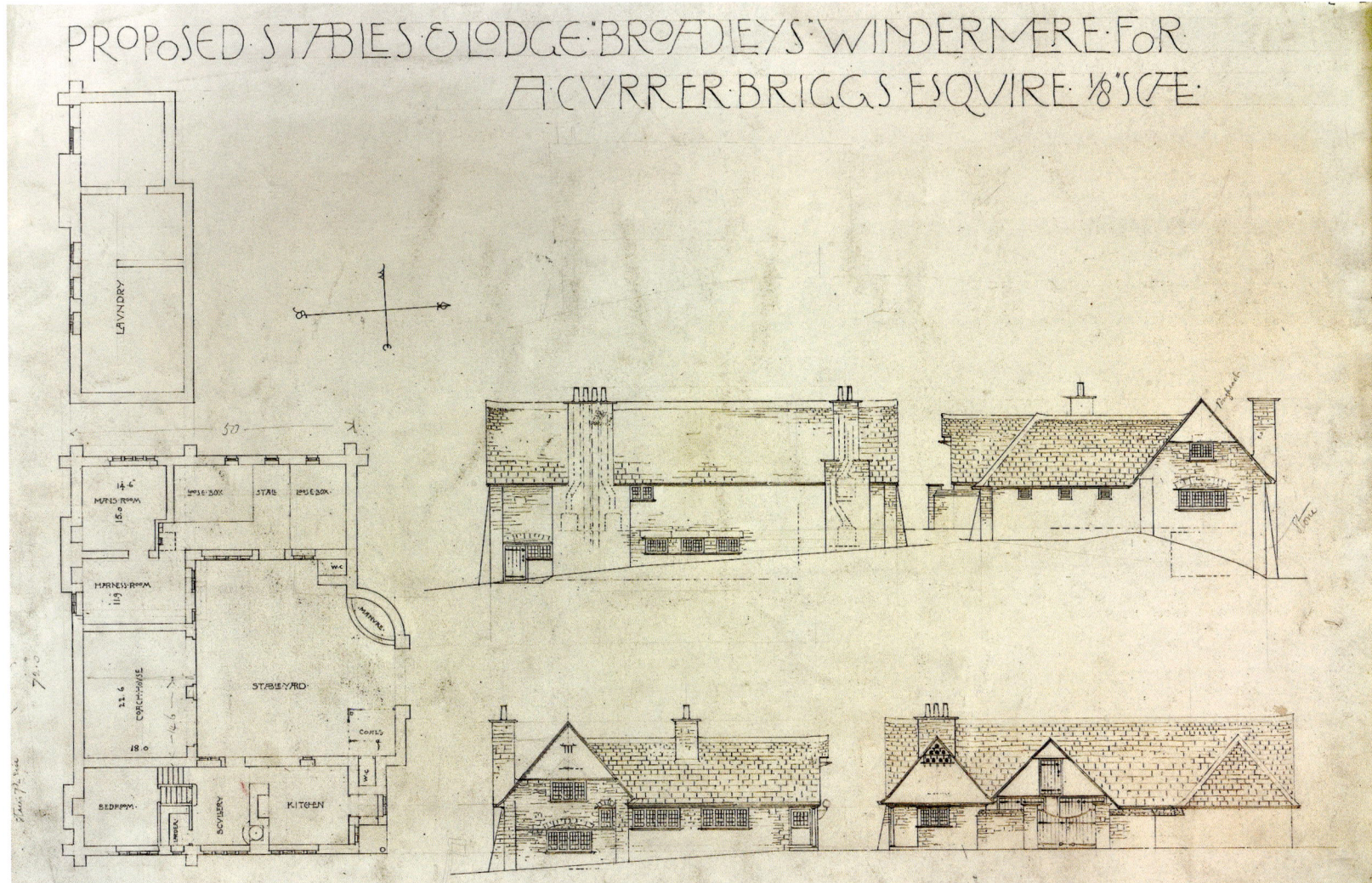

stable and coach house, which would have taken up part of the present sunken lawn. In the event the lodge only was built (Feb 26 1899, contract price £458). The detached stable (Jan 1900) may not have been built, for the age of the motorcar was upon us, and Arthur Currer Briggs was an ardent convert.

ABOVE The lodge. July 1912.

BELOW The lodge today

THE GARDEN

The presentation perspective of 1898 for Broad Leys indicates a level lawn at the south side of the house, as now. A letter from Voysey of April 1900 includes the enigmatic remark: Mr Briggs is considering the sunk garden question. The stone-walled terrace along the lake front is also shown. These suggest that Voysey designed at least the outline of the garden. The steep daffodil lawn towards the lake was there before the house, as we know from Annie Garnett. Who designed the rough paths and steps that wind between shrubberies linking the two we don't know.

Thomas Mawson is the obvious candidate, but his work is usually more formal, with balustrading, pergolas, summerhouses, and often a degree of symmetry. All of these are missing, though there was once a pergola.

Across the road was the service part of the establishment: kitchen garden and glasshouses, plus garages and a cottage for the chauffeur. English Heritage in its listing attributes the chauffeur's cottage (pictured on p.125) to Voysey. They may be right.

BELOW The garden's terraced area and steps to sundial, early 1900s

ABOVE View of the drive and garden. Sep 10 1909.

LEFT Gardens at Broad Leys, showing pergola, early 1900s

MR. BRIGGS IS CONSIDERING THE SUNK GARDEN QUESTION

BELOW View of Broad Leys with its veranda from the croquet lawn, early 1900's

RIGHT View of the garden. Sep 10 1909

BROAD LEYS IN ITS HEYDAY 1909 - 1912
BEATRIX POTTER AND HER FAMILY.

THE POTTER FAMILY OF LONDON, ALWAYS TOOK A LONG SUMMER VACATION AWAY FROM THE CITY.

Every summer Rupert and Helen Potter, and their middle-aged daughter Beatrix, plus the requisite servants (Bertram, Beatrix's brother, was away from home) took a large house generally in Scotland, and then more often the Lake District.

These houses, especially Holehird (1889 and 1895), Fawe Park and Lingholm in the Lakes, provided Beatrix with the settings for her tales. Peter Rabbit (1902) and Squirrel Nutkin (1903) were the first two, Squirrel Nutkin with a clear Lake District inspiration. They were runaway successes, indeed her publishers Warne & Co had difficulty printing enough. By 1905 she had five books in print, and had become engaged to the youngest of the Warne partners, Norman Warne. Her parents objected strongly to such a match, and it was a typically Victorian decorous engagement. But tragedy struck when Norman died, aged only 37, of leukemia.

Perhaps as a sort of escape Beatrix bought Hill Top Farm at Sawrey in 1905. The Potters were just the sort of cultivated upper middle class people who might have commissioned an elegant Arts and Crafts house, so buying a working farm was a considerable act of rebellion, incomprehensible to her parents. For the long summer holiday in 1909 and again in 1912 the family took Broad Leys. There is also some

evidence that they were here in 1910.

That second Broad Leys summer in 1912 was a critical one for Beatrix. She was in turmoil over a second proposal of marriage, this time from William Heelis, the Hawkshead agent who had handled her farm purchases. She was 46, he was 41, and it must have seemed her last chance. As with Norman Warne's proposal the couple faced a storm of opposition, but Beatrix was determined. She was also changing within herself, becoming more and more interested in farming and Westmorland life and finding less and less time for her writing, sketching and painting; becoming more like Mrs Heelis in fact, and less like the prospective Mrs. Warne. As her writing tailed off The Tale of Mr Tod (1912) and Pigling Bland (1913) were almost her last little books.

We cannot say that Broad Leys in itself was important to Beatrix. She was spending as much time as possible at Hill Top, which entailed a long walk to the ferry and another at the other end. However their stay was important to us because her father Rupert Potter was a keen and competent photographer. His beautiful photographs of the house and garden bring those far off summers back to life.

As well as those dated 1909 and 1912, there are also

LEFT   Hardwicke Rawnsley standing with Beatrix Potter outside Broad Leys *(with kind permission of the National Trust)*

some for 1910. Each one is carefully annotated on the back in pencil with the date, place and exposure. For example

Sep 8 1910
Broad Leys
R Potter
11 1/2 0 26

Among the photographs is a pleasing portrait of Beatrix and her friend Canon Hardwicke Rawnsley - the two most significant Lake District preservationists - in the porch in 1912. In another she poses with the young Norah and Joan Moore, who her diary tells us had come over to care for a hatch of little chicks in the incubator. Beatrix's illustrated letters to the six Moore children at various times are the origin of several of her tales. The Tale of Squirrel Nutkin, for instance, started life as a letter to Norah Moore.

Rupert Potter's photographs give a wonderful impression of Broad Leys in its heyday, with its beautifully fresh, pleasant, unfussy and uncluttered interiors. Much of this is due to the light linen window hangings, curtains and tablecloths, delicately embroidered with stylised flowers and mottoes. These may have been supplied by Helen's friend Annie Garnett and the Spinnery, although Kathy Haslam, recently of Blackwell, also saw the influence of the Glasgow School. A bunch of fresh flowers provides the principle decoration in each room. In one photograph appears a ghostly figure of a lady in black; Beatrix herself, perhaps. She must have walked

in briefly while the long exposure was being made.

There are many outdoor pictures too, though the lack of colour is disappointing. The garden was evidently very verdant and highly cultivated. There was a rose garden, an ornamental pond, pergola, rockery with ferns outside the north front.

A giant lily in bloom on August 2nd 1909 was cause for excitement.

Beatrix Potter and William Heelis were finally married on the 15th October 1913. In 1913 her parents had taken Lindeth Howe in Windermere. Rupert Potter's health was deteriorating, as indeed was Beatrix's own with the strain of looking after them and the conflict of wills over her marriage. Rupert died in London on the 8th of May 1914. Beatrix and William were by now living in Sawrey, struggling to keep the farm going in the war years with labour, horses, foodstuffs all in short supply. Beatrix's mother eventually moved up to Cumbria, where she was a trial to her daughter until her death. Meanwhile F. Warne & Co was in trouble. In 1917 Harold Warne was arrested for defrauding the company. Beatrix was both their largest creditor and their principal asset. In order to save what she could she put together sufficient old drawings to make up Appley Dapply's Nursery Rhymes, which came out at the end of 1917. It sold well, and was followed in 1918 by Johnny Town-Mouse. These were almost the last of her little books. Without them Warne's could not have survived.

RIGHT Original drawing room showing tiled fireplace and door opening onto the veranda. Table lamp on the far left was designed and manufactured by W.A.S. Benson as was the light on the left of the fireplace. Sep 8 1910

LEFT　**Original drawing room - further view**. Textiles and embroideries show Glasgow School influence. The larger picture above the sofa is 'The Salutation of Beatrice' (1859) by D.G. Rossetti. To the right is a detail or sketch from 'Dante's Dream' (1871), also by Rossetti. Note the grand piano in the corner of the room. July 1912

RIGHT Original drawing room. Most of the furniture in these images is by Voysey. The mirror on the far left is Glasgow School. The picture above the bookcase is Le Chant d'Amour by Edward Burne-Jones (oil on canvas 1868-73)

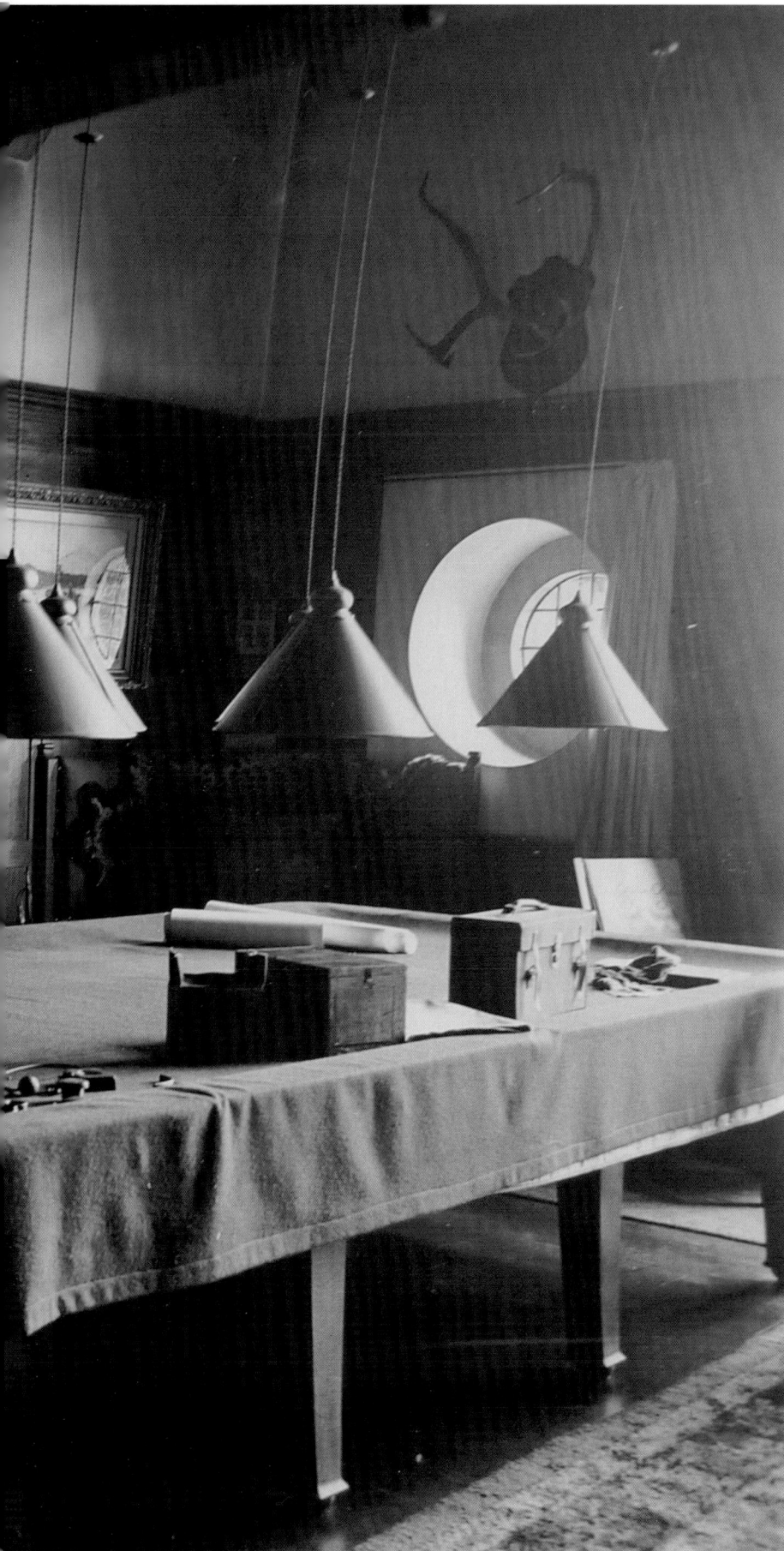

LEFT **Original hall** with snooker table. Various artwork
on the wood panelled walls. View of drawing room
though the open door. July 1909

RIGHT   Original hall showing stone inglenook fireplace. A selection of pewter plates, chargers, tankards and lidded jugs sit on the wooden mantel shelf. Sept 8 1910

RUPERT POTTER'S PHOTOGRAPHS GIVE A WONDERFUL IMPRESSION OF BROAD LEYS IN ITS HEYDAY, WITH ITS BEAUTIFULLY FRESH, PLEASANT, UNFUSSY AND UNCLUTTERED INTERIORS.

SCHMUCK IST REINLICHKEIT;

DES HAUSES GLÜCK ZUFRIEDENHEIT;

DES HAUSES SEGEN FRÖMMIGKEIT

ADORNMENT IS CLEANLINESS;

HAPPINESS OF THE HOUSE IS CONTENTMENT;

BLESSING OF THE HOUSE IS PIETY

GERMAN MOTTO EMBROIDERED ON CURTAIN PELMET
AND ITS ENGLISH TRANSLATION

LEFT **Original dining room** showing bay window with embroidered German motto on curtain pelmet. On the far right is a double heart chair designed by Voysey. The armchair in the foreground is upholstered with 'Owl' textile designed by Voysey. Sep 6 1909.

RIGHT **Original dining room - further view.** Dresser and chair with vertical splat-back designed by Voysey, as were the double heart chairs seen here. The small lidded jug on the dresser is from the Keswick School of Industrial Art. Sep 1909.

A GIANT LILY IN BLOOM ON AUGUST
2ND 1909 WAS CAUSE FOR EXCITEMENT.

ABOVE   Giant lily. Aug 2 1909

LEFT   **Another view of the dining room** at a different date - now with Voysey rug in
the centre of the room. The dining table is Cotswold School. July 1912

FOR THE LONG SUMMER HOLIDAY IN
1909 AND AGAIN IN 1912 THE FAMILY
TOOK BROAD LEYS

RIGHT **The original kitchen** with cast iron oven
range. Sep 1912

LEFT **Original main bedroom** showing tiled fireplace with wooden surround. Wallpaper and carpet by Voysey. The picture on the far left is 'Portrait of Thomas Carlyle' by J.M. Whistler. The framed work to the left of the fireplace is a portrait of Arthur Currer Briggs as Lord Mayor of Leeds (1903-04). The two smaller pieces of pottery on the mantelpiece are possibly Linthorpe or Elton Ware. Aug 29 1909

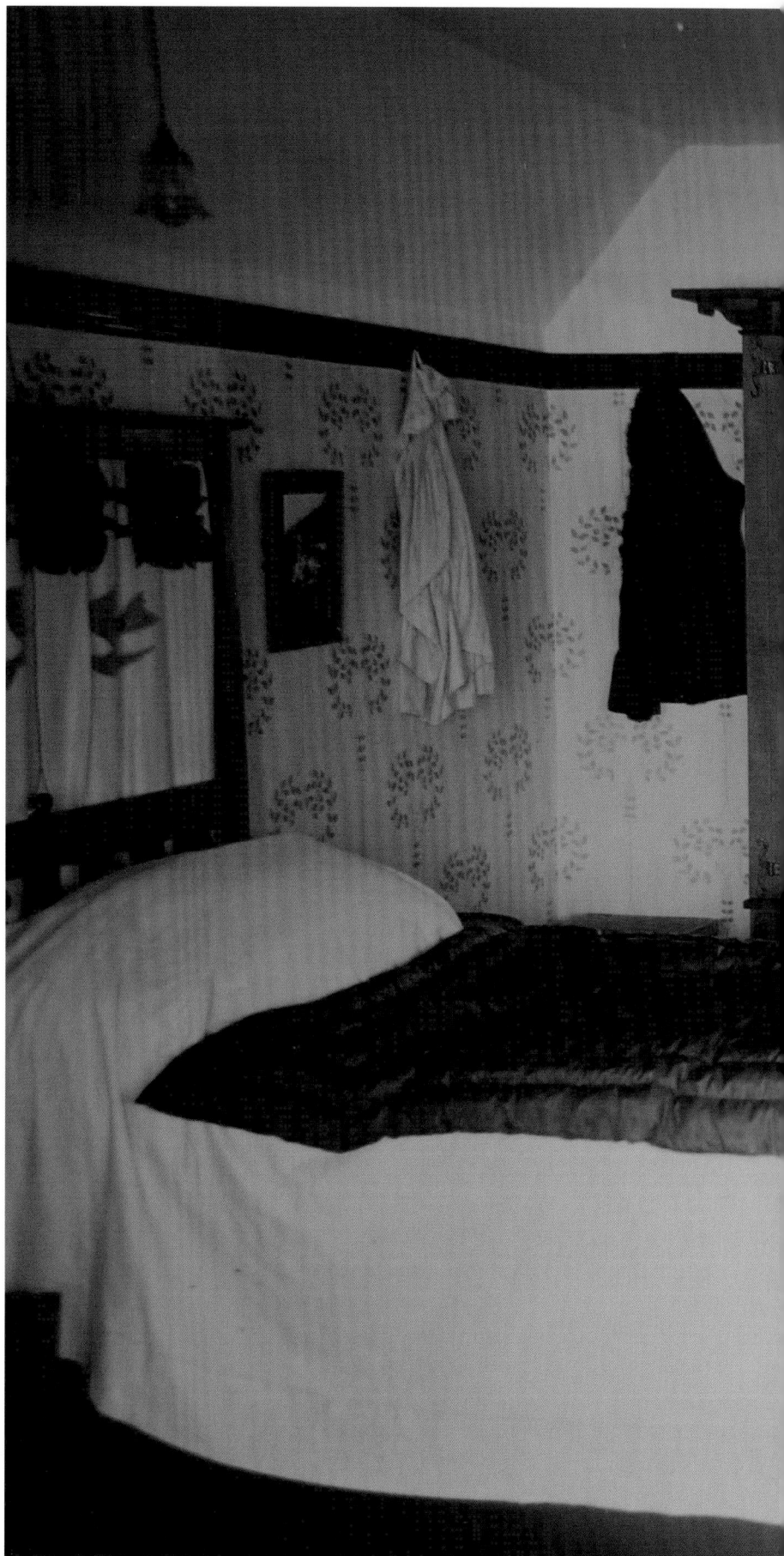

RIGHT **Original bedroom** - further view showing Voysey wallpaper and carpet, with connecting bathroom. Aug 1912

The wallpaper "Birds and Berries" was according to the catalogue record designed by Voysey for Broad Leys , but it is unfortunately not seen in any of these images.

BROAD LEYS IN A TIME OF CHANGE 1906 - 1925
HELEN CURRER BRIGGS

ARTHUR, LIKE HIS FATHER BEFORE HIM, DIED SUDDENLY, UNEXPECTEDLY, AND TOO YOUNG

LEFT Broad Leys as an auxillary hospital during World War 1

ABOVE Monument and bronze relief by Hamo Thornycroft, marking the Briggs family grave at Lawnswood Cemetery, Leeds

To explain why Broad Leys was available to let to the Potters for the whole summer we must backtrack.

On August 29th 1906 the Briggs family took their staff from Broad Leys to Tarn Hawes (spelt thus in their letters) for an open air picnic. This was intended as a thankyou for all the extra work during the Mayoral year. The next morning, the 30th, Arthur Currer Briggs set out in his new car, an open five-seater, four cylinder Ariel, to drive back to Leeds. The company's AGM, at which he was due to preside, was scheduled for the following day, the 31st. Sally, the maid, woke him as usual at 7 o'clock and gave him his hot drink of effervescing water. While she was pulling up the blinds she heard him get out of bed. He immediately tumbled over the the end of the bed and sank on the floor and died in a minute, before she could do anything. So Arthur, like his father before him, died suddenly, unexpectedly, and too young. He was only 51. Although there was a history of heart trouble his death was a terrible shock. Only two days earlier, on the day of the picnic, Arthur had written to his brother Ernest finalising the details of a planned fishing trip to Scotland. The letter is preserved, with much other memorabilia, in the Katherine Briggs archive at Leeds University. Helen his wife was telegraphed immediately, and arrived later in the day from Windermere. Meanwhile

Gerald and Geoff had to undertake the meeting; Bertie and Donald came up in the afternoon. And so the family was assembled.

The funeral was held at Mill Hill Unitarian Chapel, which the family had supported for many years, on the Tuesday following. Donald wrote 'The feeling of sorrow is intense in Leeds and there will be hundreds of people.' The Briggs family grave is in Lawnswood Cemetery, Leeds, in the Upper Woodland Glade. The bronze relief which adorns the monument is by Hamo Thornycroft, one of the great sculptors of the day. It shows The Sower, plus an angel and wreath.

After the death of her husband Helen Briggs, as she always signed herself, visited Broad Leys less often. She survived her husband by more than thirty years. Even today Helen (Nell or Nellie in family letters) comes across as a force to be reckoned with; energetic, musical, conscious of her privileges and conscientious in her duty to society. When she died in 1936, aged 77, she was given a full obituary in the Yorkshire Post. 'By far the greater part of her life was given to philanthropic works, especially on behalf of women and children.' At Whitwood colliery she saw the completion of Voysey's cottages and Institute that her husband had commissioned. In her opening speech she declared 'As it means the betterment of every man it must mean the uplifting of every

'BY FAR THE GREATER PART OF HER LIFE WAS GIVEN TO PHILANTHROPIC WORKS, ESPECIALLY ON BEHALF OF WOMEN AND CHILDREN.'

THE YORKSHIRE POST

woman and child'. In 1911 she financed the building of a village hall, which may or may not be by Voysey. It carries a fine stone plaque to the memory of her husband Arthur Currer Briggs.

Her mother-in-law Catherine, called Gran in family letters, had settled into a lakeside house close to Broad Leys at Ghyll Head. Ernest describes it in a letter (1902) to his daughter Katharine: 'the funny part of this house is that it is built right out of the water and underneath there is a boathouse where Gran keeps her two boats'. Today this is a pretty ochre washed property at the water's edge, with a miniature dock. A big room with an oriel window stands over the water. It is similar in its rambling style and low-pitched roofs to the big house now called Ghyll Head.

Granny Briggs seems to have set her daughter-in-law an example. Donald Briggs records 'Our Nannie called Cecilia Teece left to serve as matron at the summer home for 'Leeds Friendless Girls', which was at Ghyll Head, Windermere, run and financed by Grandmother.' The aim was to give the poorest children a break from their urban environment: wholesome food and healthy exercise in clean air and fine surroundings. The present use of the big house, Ghyll Head, as an outdoor centre for children from Manchester (but with a new boathouse) is highly appropriate.

LEFT   Lakeside house at Ghyll Head, home of Arthur Currer Briggs' mother Catherine

BELOW   Helen Briggs in later life

'THE FUNNY PART OF THIS HOUSE IS THAT IT IS BUILT RIGHT OUT OF THE WATER AND UNDERNEATH THERE IS A BOATHOUSE WHERE GRAN KEEPS HER TWO BOATS'

ABOVE Leeds children awaiting their trip
BELOW Boys on their way to the holiday camp

THE TIRELESS MOTHER OF TEN THOUSAND CHILDREN

LEEDS POOR CHILDREN'S HOLIDAY CAMP

The chief and lasting legacy of Arthur and Helen's mayoral year was the founding in 1904 of the Leeds Poor Children's Holiday Camp, with the same aims but a permanent home. After a temporary start at Hest Bank she acquired a site between Arnside and Silverdale, setting up a single storey wooden pavilion with a verandah which she had bought from the Bradford Exhibition for £53, plus £39 p&p.

In April 1919 this was accidentally burnt down, so no children came that year. A new building of wood and corrugated iron was put up near the old one, opening in September 1920. Helen Briggs, who visited the children frequently, was honoured in 1925 by a bronze plaque representing 'Motherhood' and inscribed 'the tireless mother of ten thousand children'. In fact it is estimated that 21,000 children had benefitted by a holiday there at the time of her death in 1936.

In 1949 this building was in turn demolished and the present one, white with flat roofs, put up. It was designed by G. Alan Burnett. While it was being built the children went to Langrigg in Bowness 'a lovely big house with double staircase'.

The children were weighed before and after their holiday, and the success of the scheme was largely gauged on the results. One boy aged 9 gained virtually a stone. Their reminiscences are not all golden. 'We were too regimentated, like a little army.' 'It was a free holiday but a rough do.' 'To me it was a penance not a holiday. We were poor at home but happy, and the time spent there was not happy. I hated the clothes we had to wear, the food, also the staff were very strict. I must not forget the toilet block, a long wooden bench with seven holes (dry of course) we called them the seven holes of misery, had a saying for each one.' Philanthropy at that time was often wielded with a somewhat heavy hand. But in

1943 Muriel Levy recalled:

'I never knew that far from town
With all its dirt and noise,
Were fields and trees and lovely spots
for little girls and boys.'

Today the place is called Silverdale Holiday Centre. After more than a century, excepting only the year 2001 when the foot and mouth epidemic prevented any visits, it serves the same purpose, offering free holidays to primary-age children who need a break. This is a double edged plaudit if you think about it - all praise to Leeds and the Holiday Centre, but a sad reflection on the state of the nation and its children. 58,000 children have stayed there since the charity started.

IT WAS A FREE HOLIDAY BUT A ROUGH DO

BELOW Helen Briggs surrounded by the children of a deprived area of Leeds

THE AIM WAS TO GIVE THE POOREST CHILDREN A BREAK FROM THEIR URBAN ENVIRONMENT: WHOLESOME FOOD AND HEALTHY EXERCISE IN CLEAN AIR AND FINE SURROUNDINGS.

AS AN AFFECTIONATE TRIBUTE
TO
HELEN CURRER BRIGGS
WHO AS LADY MAYORESS
OF LEEDS (1903 – 1904) AT
THE INCEPTION OF THE CAMP AND EVER
SINCE AS CHAIRWOMAN HAS BEEN ITS
MOST CONSTANT AND GENEROUS FRIEND
"THE TIRELESS MOTHER OF
TEN THOUSAND CHILDREN"
THIS TABLET WAS ERECTED
BY THE GENERAL COMMITTEE AND
FRIENDS OF THE CAMP
AD 1925

'I NEVER KNEW THAT FAR FROM TOWN
WITH ALL ITS DIRT AND NOISE,
WERE FIELDS AND TREES AND LOVELY SPOTS
FOR LITTLE GIRLS AND BOYS'.
MURIEL LEVY

RIGHT   Bronze plaque commissed in 1925 to honour Helen Briggs' work at the Silverdale Holiday Camp

THE FIRST WORLD WAR

The Lake District might seem to be far removed from the theatre of war, but of course it is not so. At Blackwell is a charming painting of Barbara Collingwood by her daughter Dora, painted probably at Ghyll Head. An idyllic Lake District scene. Barbara sits in the shady garden reading the newspaper, the lake gleams through the trees. The painting's title comes as a shock: 'Reading the casualty lists, circa 1914'. Joseph Holt of Blackwell was killed at Gallipoli on 4/6/1915 aged 33, as was Alexander Nicol Milne, 7/8/1915 aged 31, of the family who were soon to buy Broad Leys, and John Reginald Lingard of Holehird, 21/8/1915. All three are commemorated on the Helles Memorial in Turkey, among the 1,215 names of the Manchester Regiment.

Broad Leys during the First World War was lent and funded by Helen Briggs to serve as an auxiliary hospital to Fusehill Hospital in Carlisle. 20 officers were invalided at Broad Leys, one of them being her own son Reginald with shell shock and gas poisoning. He was nursed by 'Rouge' who became his first wife after he was discharged. They had two sons Arthur Noel and Michael Henry. Reginald married again in 1932, and had another son Richard and twin daughters Christine (Leach) and Thelma (Legge). He was only 56 when he died. Another convalescing patient was Thomas Garibaldi Farina of the Northumberland Fusiliers. Helen Briggs became his godmother in 1928.

BROAD LEYS WAS LENT AND FUNDED BY HELEN BRIGGS TO SERVE AS AN AUXILIARY HOSPITAL

ABOVE   Helen Briggs in her nurse's uniform

LEFT   Nurses outside Broad Leys, 1914 - 1918

RIGHT   Dora Altounyan's painting *Reading the casualty lists, circa 1914. (Courtesy of Abbot Hall, Kendal)*

ABOVE   Helen Briggs

LEFT   War memorial outside Mill Hill Chapel in Leeds, donated by Helen Briggs

Helen Briggs also gave the war memorial outside the Unitarian Mill Hill Chapel in Leeds. It was unveiled in 1921, as was the memorial tablet inside the church.

It might be assumed that it was the First World War which put an end to the Arts and Crafts Movement, as it did to so many things. In fact it had already died of its own accord. Although so influential and widespread it was a surprisingly short lived phenomenon. Voysey's houses were all built in the two decades straddling 1900; his architectural commissions were already drying up by 1906, and his last completed houses were designed in 1909. Yet he lived until 1941 and was an active and successful designer. A similar story can be told of the other Arts and Crafts architects, such as Prior and Lethaby, unless like Lutyens they radically changed their style. Tastes were changing, becoming less adventurous as the ample disposable incomes enjoyed by the upper middle classes were whittled away. It is significant for instance that when Walter and Dorothy Milne built themselves a house in Alderley Edge in 1912 - Walter was the brother of Jack Milne who bought Broad Leys - it was primly neo-Georgian. What makes it striking is that their architect, Percy Scott Worthington, had built a pukka Arts and Crafts house called Ashley Green in the Lakes only a few years earlier.

IT MIGHT BE ASSUMED THAT IT WAS THE FIRST WORLD WAR WHICH PUT AN END TO THE ARTS AND CRAFTS MOVEMENT, AS IT DID TO SO MANY THINGS. IN FACT IT HAD ALREADY DIED OF ITS OWN ACCORD.

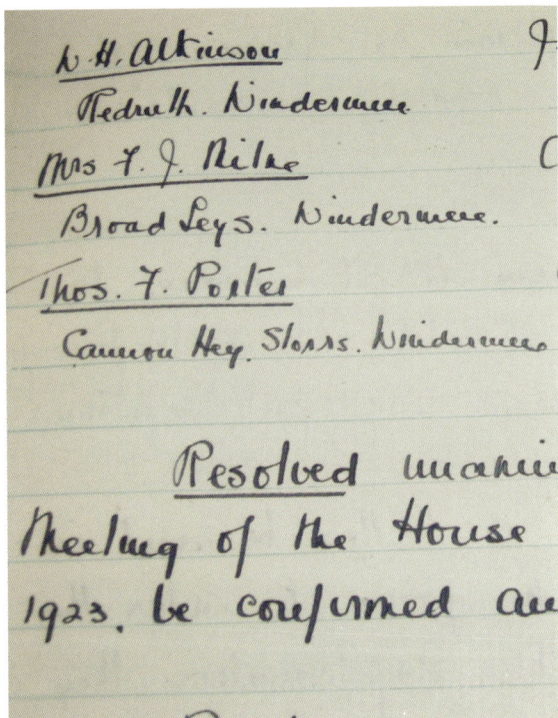

THE MILNE FAMILY APPEAR
FREQUENTLY IN THE RECORDS OF
WINDERMERE GOLF CLUB

THE MILNES WERE TO OWN BROAD
LEYS UNTIL 1950.

AFTER THE WAR

Broad Leys was sold. A conveyance dated 23rd August 1920 records the sale by Helen Currer Briggs to Arthur Brook Aspland for £12,000. Aspland was director and manager of Slack Mills Ltd (cotton) of Godley and Hyde in East Manchester. His memorial is in Hyde Chapel, Gee Cross (presumably Crowther's Unitarian church). In 1919 he presented the family house, Werneth Lodge, to the corporation. It is now a residential home.

He did not keep Broad Leys for long, although records of the Golf Club show that he kept up his Windermere connections. On 8th January 1923 he sold Broad Leys for £11,500. Aspland moved to Brackenrigg, Windy Hill Road, Bowness. He died some time after 1940.

The new owner was Frederick John Milne (Jack), whose address is given (Golf Club 1922) as Abbotsfield, Malvern. The Milnes were to own Broad Leys until 1950.

Jack Milne was the grandson of James Milne, born in 1804, joint founder of the Kendal Milne department store in Manchester. Their Manchester home was Belmont House, near Cheadle, of 1864. It is a pleasant stuccoed house with a central doorcase, two shallow bow windows, and flanking wings. The architect was Alfred Waterhouse, no less; architect of Manchester Town Hall and Strangeways prison.

Thomas Dewhurst Milne, his eldest son, took over over the department store (Faulkner had dropped out), and married Lucy. They had four sons, of whom Frederick John (Jack) was the eldest. He married Minnie, and in due course they bought Broad Leys. The other brothers were Walter, Alexander Nicol, and Malcolm. Alexander was killed in the First World War.

The Milne family appear frequently in the records of Windermere Golf Club, not just W.J. but also his wife Minnie who was Lady Captain in 1949, his brother Walter (W.H.) and Walter's wife Dorothy. So do four Milne children - W.G. and Joan, both of Dawstone i.e. Walter and Dorothy's children, and John and Miss J. (Jill) both of Broad Leys.

It looks as though Walter and Dorothy, the builders of Penn in Alderley Edge, bought Dawstone in 1923 following the death of its builder Alexander Millington Sing (Synge) of Liverpool. Dawstone is another notable Arts and Crafts house, built in 1903 to a design by Dan Gibson and extended in 1912 by W.L Dolman.

Perhaps we can infer that the two brothers and their families were close. The two Milne families evidently had a liking for high quality architecture and fine craftsmanship. And golf!

The Kendal Milne store was taken over by Harrods in 1919, and in 1920 Belmont House with 22.5 acres was sold to The Together Trust - Boys' and Girls' Welfare Society - to create the Children's Garden Village. The Milnes in Mancunian philanthropic style funded the Trust's sanatorium. Belmont House itself is still there on Schools Hill, now the Together Trust's retirement home.

ABOVE Mrs.F.J.Milne of Broad Leys
(Courtesy of Windermere Golf Club)
RIGHT Belmont House, near Cheadle, Cheshire

THE WINDERMERE MOTOR BOAT CLUB 1925 - 1951

'WHEN LIKE MINDS COME TOGETHER TO PURSUE THEIR SPORTING AIMS A CLUB IS NECESSARY FOR FULFILLMENT.'

LEFT The final photograph taken at the clubhouse at Bowness Bay

BELOW Plans and elevation for proposed original clubhouse in 1926

'How fast can yours go?' 'Faster than yours'. Informal races between the early motor boats were a regular feature of Windermere in the years following the First World War, but as their speeds and popularity increased something more organised and more sociable was needed. On the 24th of October 1925 a group of eight enthusiasts met at Riggs (now Windermere Hotel) to found a club. The stated aim was 'to promote motor boat racing and to regulate safety on the lake'. And so the Windermere Motor Boat Club was born.

The founder members at that first meeting included Harold (E.H.) Pattinson, who took the chair, Mr. R.R. Rothwell of Broomriggs near Hawkshead, J.C. Aitchison, and R.B. Stephens. The formation of the club was the only business on that first day, but further meetings on 21 November and 5 December hammered out the details. W.J. McVey was appointed treasurer and secretary at £25 p.a., a position which he held for over thirty years. Others joined, and 43 members were listed in 1926. Amongst them are O. Gnosspelius and H.B. Wakefield, whom we have met earlier over the amphibious plane duel. The club subscription was set at 3 guineas for gentlemen plus a 2 guinea entrance fee, 1 guinea for ladies.

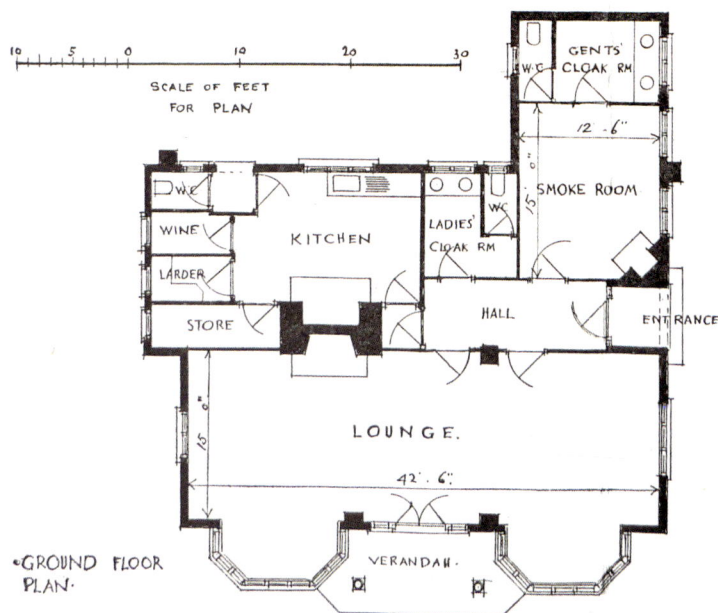

GROUND FLOOR PLAN.

ABOVE *Canfly*, 1926

Back, left to right: Hugh Tevis, Jack Brook, EH Pattinson.

Front, left to right: RR Rothwell, JC Aitchison, Miss Carstairs, Arthur Bray

A prospectus (preserved at the club) was printed for a meeting on January 16th 1926, held also at Riggs. By now Pattinson had been elected Commodore, John C. Aitchison Vice Commodore. The prospectus includes plans and elevations (presumably drawn up by Pattinsons the builders) for a proposed clubhouse, to be built on a site in Bowness Bay.

Something else was needed as a stopgap until this could come into being. The father of one of the first members, Ronnie Stephens, came to the rescue with the loan of his boathouse near Shepherd's Yard in Bowness Bay, and this was duly opened as a makeshift clubhouse on 1st May 1926. It was a two-span building, with a wet dock in one half, the other serving as a meeting room with a bay window overlooking the lake.

However, this could only be a temporary arrangement. In 1927 a company was formed to buy a piece of land near the Glebe on Bowness Bay. The cost was £550. By the end of the year sufficient further money had been raised - it was hard work - to build a prefabricated timber clubhouse (i.e. not the 1926 prospectus design) and a pier, at a total cost of £1,422. This served 'to provide a pleasant waterside clubhouse with catering facilities and ample accommodation for cars and boats' for the next quarter of a century, and its three-bay wooden verandah features in many early photographs.

THE STATED AIM WAS 'TO PROMOTE MOTOR BOAT RACING AND TO REGULATE SAFETY ON THE LAKE'

MISS CARSTAIRS, 'AN ECCENTRIC CROSS-DRESSING TOMBOY MILLIONAIRESS', WAS A SERIOUS ENTHUSIAST

RACING

Thirteen races were arranged in that first year. The boats raced were substantial, handbuilt, wooden craft, including some single-step hydroplanes, with inboard engines. They were elegant looking boats, of white-painted or varnished mahogany with smooth teak decking, with a sharp vertical bow and transome. The big engine was usually amidships under sliding covers, and the crew generally sat well aft or even right at the back.

The first race was held on 22nd May 1926. Eight competitors took part but conditions were not good, and in rough water and in poor visibility there was no clear winner. Two days later eleven boats took part in a scratch race. This time the race was more successful, and was won by Betty Carstairs in her boat Newg. '1926 Miss M.B. Carstairs' is therefore the very first name to appear on the club honours boards. This is a little ironical, for the club was essentially a male affair, with reduced membership rates for ladies - indeed, she was not yet a member. However Miss Carstairs, 'an eccentric cross-dressing tomboy millionairess', was a serious enthusiast, the ace driver between the wars. Newg ZK10 as can be seen in old photographs was a powerfully businesslike boat with the crew hunched right at the back.

BELOW Betty Carstairs in her boat Newg, 1926

On that occasion Harold Pattinson in his boat came second. We can still see Canfly, because it is preserved; a sleek and handsome 28ft mahogany launch, built by Harry Breaker in 1922 to take a huge 1917 Rolls Royce Hawk aero-engine from an airship. *Canfly* was built for speed, and is apparently a pig to manoeuvre and handle. Typical speeds of the day are indicated by a Westmorland Gazette report that on 17th July 1926 R.B. Stephens' Eris did 34 m.p.h. over a 3 hour race, with one passenger.

In 1927 most races had 10-15 participants. By 1929 it could be as many as 36. Racing took place over two courses, each 7 1/2 miles long: one in the north basin between Henholme and Waterhead, the other in the south basin between Storrs and Blakeholme.

These early motor boats were professionally maintained. Borwick's mechanics would come down and get everything ready. The owners didn't get their hands dirty - white flannels, jacket and tie were de rigeur. This was carried to a fine art by owners such

THE OWNERS DIDN'T GET THEIR HANDS DIRTY - WHITE FLANNELS, JACKET AND TIE WERE DE RIGEUR.

LEFT E.H. Pattinson and *Canfly*

ABOVE EH Pattinson on *Canfly*, with its Rolls Royce engine

BELOW 1938, ChrisCraft *Jane* at the Wateredge
(Courtesy of Windermere Steamboat Museum)

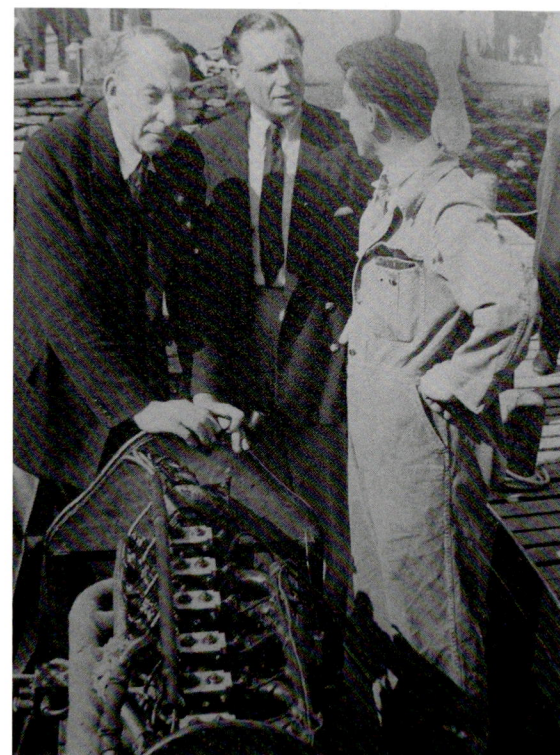

ABOVE 29th July 1939. No 7 *Merrit* Charles Hanson overtaking No 16 *Diana* (Miss Beryl Pritchard), Whippet Class Championship

THE FIRST RACE WAS HELD ON 22ND MAY 1926. EIGHT COMPETITORS TOOK PART BUT CONDITIONS WERE NOT GOOD, AND IN ROUGH WATER AND IN POOR VISIBILITY THERE WAS NO CLEAR WINNER.

as Henry Segrave or Dicky Booker who might roll up in a Bentley just a few minutes before starting time. Immaculately dressed, cigar in mouth, they would step straight into the boat, and off! No lifejackets, no rescue boats.

A relic of those days was Fitting Out Dinner, at which owners entertained their crews. This was the only time the mechanics were made welcome socially, and until recently it was a gents only affair with much serious drinking. Lady members, however successful as racing drivers, were not permitted. A similar situation pertained at the Royal Windermere Yacht Club (RWYC) - where indeed lady owners were not allowed in the clubhouse at all. Their prizes had to be collected by surrogate gentlemen.

By the 1930s the club was going from strength to strength. It was in some respects a golden age, at any rate for some. The British got out and about in their new cars to explore the countryside, equipped with camera and Shell guide. Roads were improved, among them in 1926 the lakeside road outside

Broad Leys, which was originally the private drive to Storrs with a lodge at each end. Pattinsons and other builders were busy with new houses, often taking their design cue from Broad Leys and Moor Crag. Elsewhere in the industrial north however the Depression was biting hard. Not far away, towns such Barrow, Workington and Maryport were particularly hard hit by the industrial downturn. From 1919 to 1927 Barrow was virtually bankrupt, as the market for iron and steel collapsed and too many shipyards chased too few orders. It was, with hindsight, an unstable period.

New types of boat were appearing, gradually superseding the heavy handbuilt craft of the 1920s. The American ChrisCraft, the local-built Whippet, the Albatross and the Delta all made their appearance. Lady Craven, from a shipbuilding dynasty in Barrow in Furness, was in 1933 racing a Chris Craft called Moana.

The Whippet was a small, light, 1 1/2 litre inboard engine timber hydroplane built at Borwicks and

Agnews. The war interrupted their development and no more appeared after the war. Later, local boatdesigner and builder Charlie Gardener of Anchorage Boats built some 1800cc Volvo engine hydroplanes which were purchased by club members. They were also destined for a short racing life, the Anchorage boathouse in Nab Wood Bay was burnt down, the plans and patterns for the emerging class were lost; no more were built. There is an example in the Museum.

These classic speedboats are still valued, including several owned by club members. They can be admired at an annual regatta in August, and a smart Chris Craft of 1938 called Jane, K64, can be seen at the Windermere Steamboat Museum. Jane, a 2-seater built in Florida, with a 6-cylinder engine and capable of 35 mph, was exhibited at the 1938 Motor Show. Acquired by E.H. Pattinson and brought to Windermere, she was used for Home Guard duties during the war but, some time afterwards was taken south by Viscount Cross. G.H. Pattinson returned her to Windermere for the collection.

Those heady days can be aptly summarised by the story of White Lady II. It had long been realised that the long narrow hulls of early speedboats, designed to slice through the waves, tended to sink still lower in the water at high speed. A flat bottom with hard chines was better, and a transverse break underneath helped the boat to unstick and plane on top of the water rather than through it.

White Lady II was built in the winter of 1930-31 at Hythe, and in 1936 was bought by Derek Tinker and J.E. Lumb and brought up to Windermere. She incorporated the latest thinking, with three steps or breaks underneath. The engine was mounted backwards, with a V-drive gearbox between the two crew cockpits. She was fast, with a top speed of 55 m.p.h. In 1937, in the middle of a race, White Lady suddenly started to fill with water. Luckily Tinker's wife was nearby in Rita; Derek managed to step coolly onto Rita, as White Lady went down stern first into 120 ft of water. This happened off Rawlinson's Nab, opposite Broad Leys. Tinker went back to the clubhouse in Bowness Bay, dried himself off and changed, and went on to win Lady Craven's trophy in the afternoon.

ABOVE *White Lady II* recovered from the mud in 1982
BELOW *White Lady II* in action, 1936

White Lady was recovered from the mud where she lay, bows-up, in 1982. Her mahogany hull was found to be basically sound, and the engine, astonishingly, still turned. She can be seen, restored in running order, at the Steamboat Museum.

By February 1939, when Harold Pattinson once again became commodore, the prospects for the club were looking good. Membership stood at 44 gentlemen and 12 ladies. Racing speeds were increasing. An official race programme for 29 July 1939 provides a snapshot of this hopeful period. It was the first to include a one-class race, the North of England 1 1/2 litre Whippet Class Championship.

'This meeting, the first of its kind to be held on Lake Windermere for many years, will, it is hoped, be an annual fixture and one which will be considered of importance in the National calendar of motor boat racing in the future'.

Start and finish were at Storrs Hall pier. There were three races:

- **Whippet Class championship 1 1/2 litre.** 'The only scratch class British built inboard engined hydroplane racing consistently at the present time.' Nine boats entered.
- **Open Scratch.** 'Entries in this event consist of ultra fast hydroplanes and it is expected that speeds of over 70mph will be exceeded.' There were seven entries. It was won by H.C. Notley in a Ventnor hydroplane at 44.5 mph average, 60 mph maximum.
- **All comers handicap.** 4 1/2 laps of the course as shown on the map. The boats were variously capable of speeds from 30 to 70 mph, so they were handicapped and started at different times in order to finish together.

But the racing season was never completed....

ABOVE   *White Lady II* back on the water in July 1984 pictured at the Windermere Steamboat Museum

BELOW   North of England, 1.5 Litre Championship, 1939

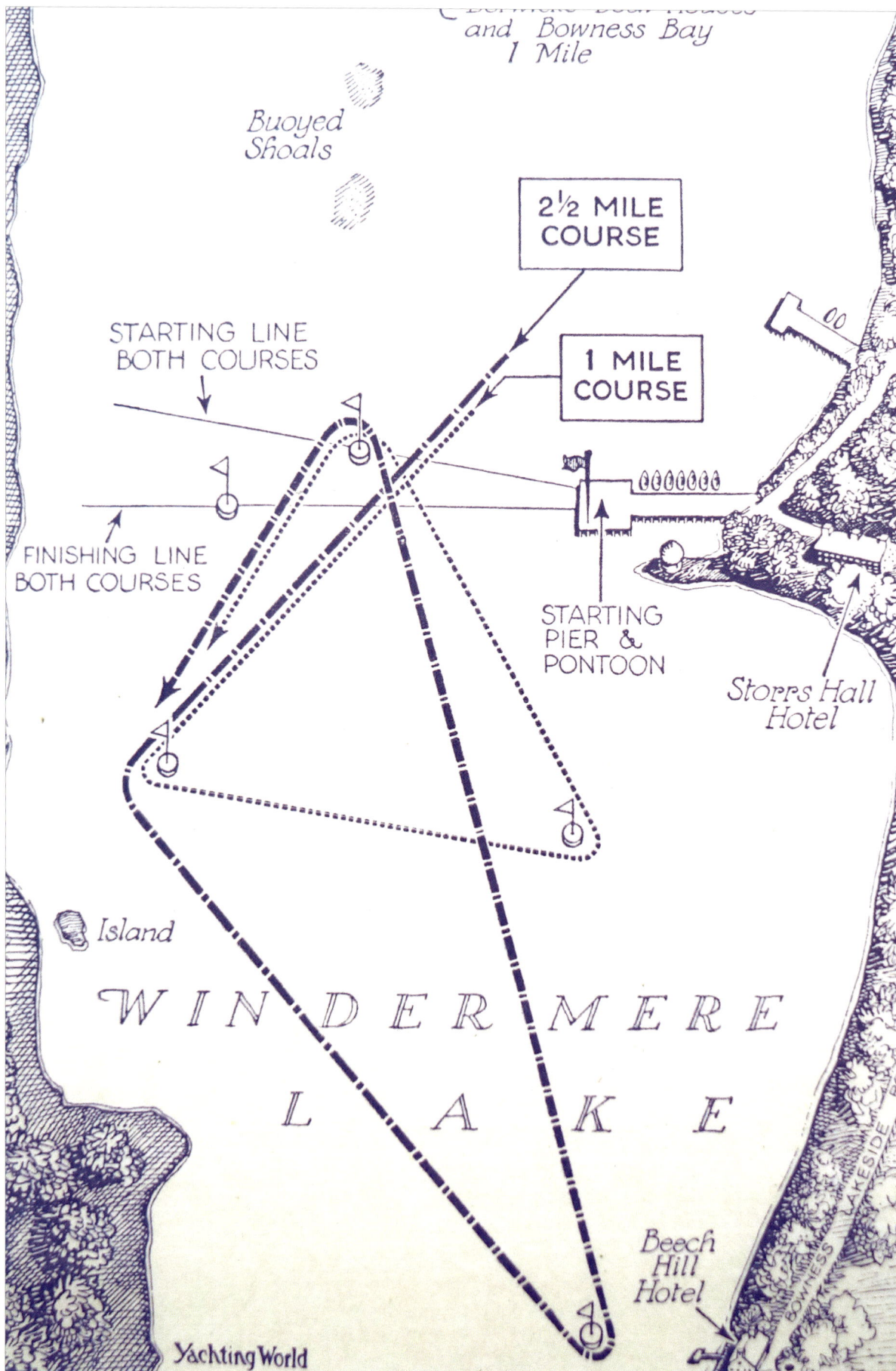

2½ MILE COURSE

1 MILE COURSE

Bowmere Boat Houses and Bowness Bay 1 Mile

Buoyed Shoals

STARTING LINE BOTH COURSES

FINISHING LINE BOTH COURSES

STARTING PIER & PONTOON

Storrs Hall Hotel

Island

W I N D E R M E R E

L A K E

Beech Hill Hotel

Yachting World

'THIS MEETING, THE FIRST OF ITS KIND TO BE HELD ON LAKE WINDERMERE FOR MANY YEARS, WILL, IT IS HOPED, BE AN ANNUAL FIXTURE AND ONE WHICH WILL BE CONSIDERED OF IMPORTANCE IN THE NATIONAL CALENDAR OF MOTOR BOAT RACING IN THE FUTURE'.

LEFT   Plan of the July 29th 1939 race meeting course showing 1 mile and 2.5 mile courses

BEATRIX POTTER'S COMMENT FROM SAWREY IS AN INTERESTING ONE IN VIEW OF HER EARLIER OPPOSITION: 'THE SILENCE OF THE STARRY SKY HAS BEEN INTERRUPTED BY AEROPLANES WHICH AT FIRST WE DETESTED AS AN INTRUSION, BUT SINCE THE WAR WE DELIGHT TO SEE THEM'.

THE SECOND WORLD WAR

'1940-1946 --- no racing'. The Second World War is recorded thus as a laconic six-year blank on the club honours board. The WMBC, like the RWYC at Bowness, stopped racing but did not close. The clubhouse remained open for members. Drinks however, like almost everything else, were rationed. The Lake District was spared all except accidental wartime damage, but Barrow shipyards were a prime target for bombing, and the flares and fires could be seen in the distance. Windermere town filled up with evacuees, especially in 1939-40, although as time went by they tended to drift back home, thinking no doubt as townies that it was better to be bombed than bored.

An interesting sequel to the Waterbird story earlier occurred when a factory was established at White Cross Bay to build and repair Short Sunderland flying boats. The Sunderland was a massive heavy-looking, four-engined aircraft with a deep fuselage. It was initially developed in the 1930s for the postal service. As redesigned for combat it was especially useful in the Battle of the Atlantic. 35 of the Mark III aircraft were built here at Windermere, out of a total of 461. Beatrix Potter's comment from Sawrey is an interesting one in view of her earlier opposition: 'The silence of the starry sky has been interrupted by aeroplanes which at first we detested as an intrusion, but since the war we delight to see them'.

ABOVE   Early powerboats at Waterhead, late 1940s

RIGHT   Frank Lydall's boat *Cheetah*, late 1940s

AFTER THE WAR PETROL RATIONING
GRADUALLY EASED AND RACING
ACTIVITIES WERE FULLY ESTABLISHED
AGAIN

After the war things gradually returned to normal, though rationing was still in place. Three races were held in 1946. It is recorded that eight boats were ready to race, including A. Roby Jones's *Robrina*, Harold Pattinson's *Jane* and W.M. Lydall's *Scud*. A few more joined them in 1947. Petrol rationing gradually eased and racing activities were fully established again and increasing. In 1949 the WMBC, against a background of continuing shortages, organised a first International Meeting. By now membership had reached 99, of which 28 were ladies and 32 were boat owners.

The 1926 clubhouse was becoming too small. Bowness Bay was increasingly crowded, and so was Bowness itself, making car parking more and more difficult. The success of that first international race meeting gave the club the extra confidence needed for the next step. Prominent on the honours boards from 1947 are N.H. Buckley and F.B. Lydall. These two names dominate the club, racing and records, over the next few years.

BELOW Racing in the 1930s

RIGHT Art Hatch in a three point proprider *Costa Livin* and Norman H. Buckley in *Miss Windermere II*

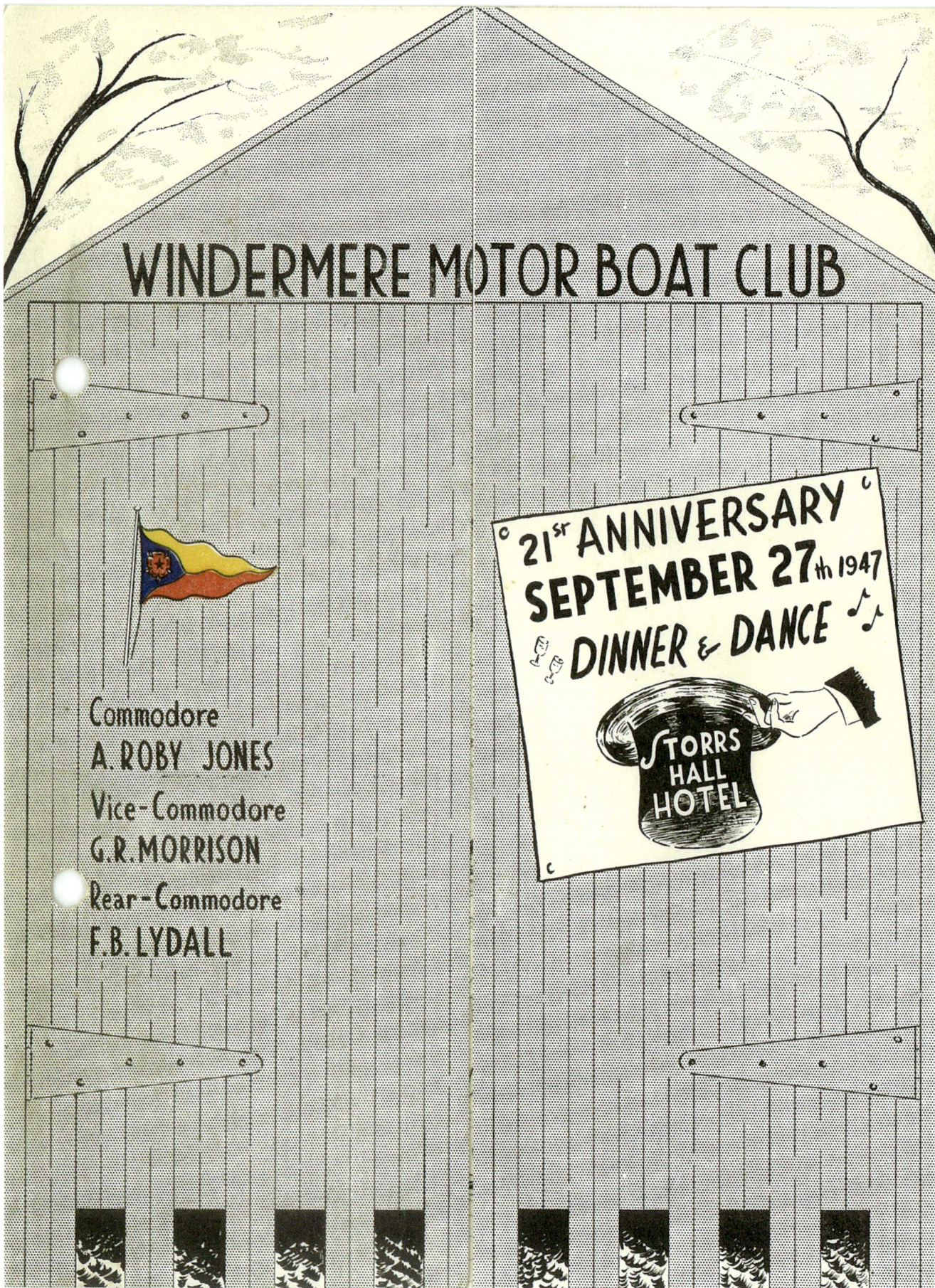

LEFT 21st Anniversary Dinner Dance invitation 1947

RIGHT Sketch found inside the invitation featuring caricatures of WMBRC members:

Wanderer - G.R. Morrison;

28 - E.H. Pattinson;

32, *The Brat* - P.K. Potter;

15, *Moonbeam* - N.H. Buckley;

69, *Cheetah* - F.B. Lydall;

33 - W.M. Lydall;

27, *Robrina* - A. Roby Jones;

17, *Jitterbug* - D. Senior;

6, *Victory* - J.I. Morrison;

9 - Mrs V. Lydall;

23, *Leander* - K. Buckley

The scoreboard reads:

9	SCUD
6	VICTORY
17	JITTERBUG
27	ROBRINA
32	THE BRAT
33	SLIP STREAM
24	OVERDRIVE
28	JANE
69	CHEETAH
23	LEANDER
15	MOONBEAM

WMBRC AT BROAD LEYS 1951 ONWARDS

WITH THE ACQUISITION OF BROAD LEYS THE WINDERMERE MOTOR BOAT CLUB HAD BECOME THE OWNERS OF ONE OF THE FINEST AND BEST-KNOWN HOUSES OF THE ARTS AND CRAFTS ERA, ON A PRIME SPOT WITH SPACIOUS GROUNDS AND AN AMPLE LAKESIDE SHORELINE.

In 1950 Broad Leys was on the market. Frederick John (Jack) Milne had died in 1948, and the house was reluctantly put up for sale by his widow, Minnie Elizabeth and their daughter Jill. The WMBC put in an offer of £15,250 - a very favourable price - on 18 May 1950. The property comprised house, lodge, wet dock boathouse (in poor condition), and 22.75 acres of land on both sides of the road, together with three cottages, garages, greenhouses, kitchen gardens and an area of woodland.

Sale particulars tell us that the lodge was then occupied by Mr. G. Clark, gardener. Over the road, in the pair of brick-built, white-rendered houses were Mr W.H. Martindale (gardener) and Mrs H. Troughton. In the 'concrete block type bungalow' - much more attractive than it sounds, and quite possibly designed by Voysey - was Mr A.W. Powell, the chauffeur. Beyond this are the garages and workshop. They are all still there.

LEFT   One of the early posters produced by Graham Loney and David Taylor to advertise the Classic Boat Rally at Broad Leys

RIGHT   The chauffeur's 'bungalow', possibly designed by Voysey

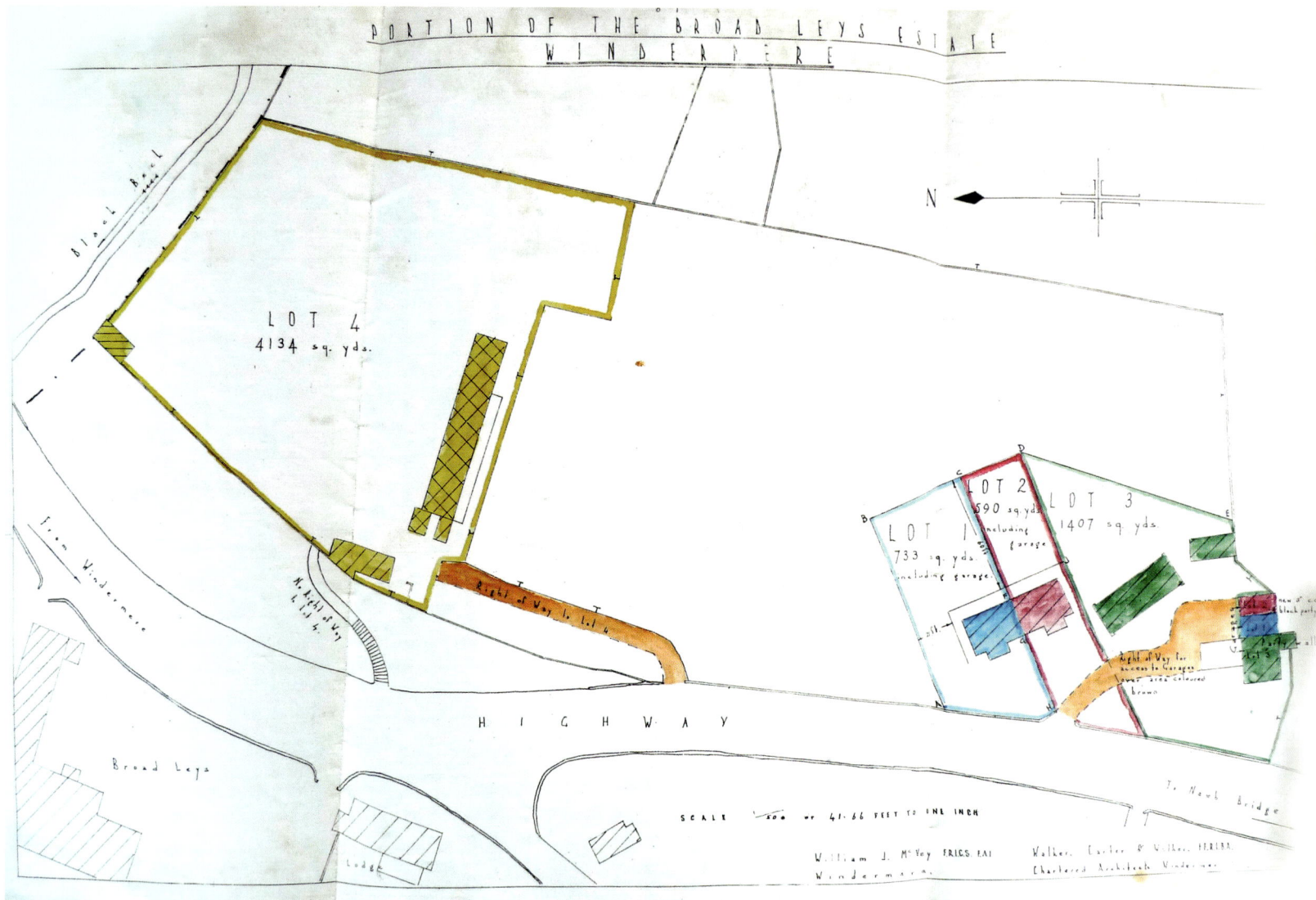

ABOVE A portion of the Broad Leys estate, put up for auction in Sept 1950.

At an Extraordinary General Meeting on 29 May 1950 the commodore, Clem Haworth, and Norman Buckley put forward the resolution to buy it. The offer was accepted and the deal was completed on 18th August 1950.

The club holds a rather poignant letter dated September 1950 from Minnie Milne who wrote to the treasurer Mr McVey from Stone House, Westmancote, Nr Tewkesbury. She acknowledges three cheques, and concludes by saying rather sadly that she wouldn't see Broad Leys again, but offering best wishes to the club in its new clubhouse.

It was a big effort to raise the money, involving loans of £500 - £50 from individual members, and the raising of an £11,500 overdraft, but it paid off handsomely in the long run. The kitchen garden and cottages over the road, put up to auction on 22 September 1950, realised a total of £10,550. The old clubhouse in Bowness Bay was subsequently sold to Borwick's for £5,500 (and demolished circa 1975). In 1958 a further slice of land south of the lodge and down to the lake was sold for £1,500.

With the acquisition of Broad Leys the Windermere Motor Boat Club had become the owners of one of the finest and best-known houses of the Arts and Crafts era, on a prime spot with spacious grounds and an ample lakeside shoreline. On 10 Feb 1951,

AT AN EXTRAORDINARY GENERAL MEETING ON 29 MAY 1950 THE COMMODORE, CLEM HAWORTH, AND NORMAN BUCKLEY PUT FORWARD THE RESOLUTION TO BUY BROAD LEYS. THE OFFER WAS ACCEPTED AND THE DEAL WAS COMPLETED ON 18TH AUGUST 1950.

ABOVE View of Broad Leys showing croquet lawn and veranda, circa 1950

ON 10 FEB 1951, AT THE 25TH AGM AND THE FIRST AT THE NEW CLUBHOUSE, THE WORD RACING WAS ADDED TO THE CLUB'S TITLE, CHANGING WMBC TO WMBRC 'TO EMPHASISE THE TRUE NATURE OF THE CLUB'.

at the 25th AGM and the first at the new clubhouse, the word Racing was added to the club's title, changing WMBC to WMBRC 'to emphasise the true nature of the club'.

Once Broad Leys was purchased, racing was concentrated in the south basin. In 1951 a second International Meeting was held. The top Windermere boats were Norman Buckley's Miss Windermere II and E.C. Giles's Diana, both of which could do 70-80mph. But the eye-opening performers were two Canadian entries, J.W. Langmuir's Running Wild and Art Hatch's Costa

Livin. They were noticeably smaller but more brutal-looking machines, 'all engine on a skimming teatray'. Costa Livin won the Duke of York trophy, Running Wild the Daily Telegraph 800 k.g. class.

Norman Buckley and Donald Campbell competed successfully at the International on Lake Garda in 1951, with Leo Villa and Arthur Henderson as engineers. In 1956 Buckley achieved 79.66 mph in Miss Windermere III, and in 1957 Miss Windermere III competed - unsuccessfully this time - in the 800 k.g. class at Lugano.

From the late forties to early sixties racing was dominated by the larger custom built timber boats with huge inboard engines including some U.S.A. built Chris Craft race boats. In the early sixties these boats began to give way to much lighter and faster sports and racing boats

Socially the club was a mixture of old and new as well. The old mould was breaking. Several important early members died or left at this time, including E.H. Pattinson who died in 1960, as did William McVey in 1961, respectively the first Commodore and Hon Secretary, and John Village in 1964. N.H.

Buckley resigned from the General Committee in 1972 but remained as Race Committee Chairman until 1973; he died in 1974. Younger people were joining, less affluent - though motorboat racing still requires cash, and always will. But by now the old wooden boats with inboard engines had all but disappeared, apart from Eddie Wade buying a timber Tremlett and Ian McMillan commissioning a timber boat which was built locally.

The little Albatrosses and Deltas were just making an appearance using aluminium, a new material for Windermere race boats.

LEFT Boats at Broad Leys jetties mid 1950s
BELOW Racing on Windermere

SOUVENIR PROGRAMME

INTERNATIONAL
MEETING
at
LAKE WINDERMERE

FRIDAY & SATURDAY · OCTOBER 5th & 6th
1951

ORGANISING CLUB
WINDERMERE MOTOR BOAT RACING CLUB

2'6

LEFT Souvenir programme of the International Meeting at Broad Leys, 1951

RIGHT International Meeting, Oct 1951. Two Canadian entries; J.W. Langmuir in *Running Wild*, a hallet hull with Orval Smith 200bhp engine and H.A. Hatch in *Costa Livin*, a Thompson hull and Townsend 200bhp engine.

They were powered by marinised Ford and Coventry Climax engines in several states of tune and no gearboxes, Geoff Lambert's Springbok and Ken Evins' Skip IV in 1967 being examples. The annual August Classic Motor Boat Rally provides the opportunity for these and many other classic boats to again grace the lake – see Broad Leys today.

In 1960 a new jetties, timing pier and boathouse were built at Broad Leys which can be seen in many photographs of the day and a new generation of boats and race drivers was about to emerge. The present well-equipped timing pier, incorporating toilets, showers and a kitchen as well as the Race

Control room, was built in 1995. The work being necessitated by the roof to the 1960 timing pier having been blown off in a terrific gale and dumped, some yards away, upside down on the foreshore and a deal of damage caused to the remaining structure.

Since 1926 the club had only allowed inboard engines. In 1965 the decision was made, after a demonstration by Bill Shakespeare and Bill Picton in Shakespeare's deep V fibreglass outboard boats which ran rings round the club boats, to allow outboards. The first, Padalin, was built by George Lewthwaite for David Fairhurst and powered by a straight 6 Mercury. Padalin was a fairly substantial timber built

LEFT   Club race start in front of Broad Leys, mid 1950s
BELOW   Club members in the timing pier

FROM THE LATE FORTIES
TO EARLY SIXTIES RACING
WAS DOMINATED BY THE
LARGER CUSTOM BUILT
TIMBER BOATS WITH HUGE
INBOARD ENGINES

boat and was shortly followed by Richard Solomon's Sheba then George Mould's Cindy, two light weight 14 ft fibreglass V hulled Bristol boats with two cylinder Carniti outboard engines.

The small Bristol boats had difficulties negotiating the wake from the bigger wooden boats, but they were faster and they didn't need a mechanic. 16 ft Bristol fibreglass and the 16 ft timber Levis of Richard Solomon (Salome) and Nick Hudddleston (Septimus) and later Jimmy Lumsdon Taylor (Omo) followed. Early 16 ft Bristols were owned by Richard Solomon (Sheba), Peter White (Au Poil) and Martin Dennison (Blue –Tu). Sheba and Septimus both became record breakers.

Four or five years after the fiberglass boats, the first racing catamarans, such as Tony Fahey's Lucy Locket (1973) and M.T. Denison's Slippery Sam (1974), came on the scene. The introduction of the tunnel-hulled cats changed the complexion of racing. They were faster and lighter, skipping over the water and highly manoeuverable, but were less able to deal with rough conditions, wash etc. In 1970 the Thames International Race had had to be cancelled because of massive rafts of driftwood - a common problem on the river at that time. Thanks to the initiative of Norman Buckley and John Reed of the Lancashire club the Queen Mother allowed the terms of the gold Duke of York Trophy to be altered to admit winners from any country not just from Britain and the Commonwealth. This provided a magnificent trophy for the first of a series of Windermere International Grand Prix. The first was held on 23 October 1971. It was a major new venture, run jointly by WMBRC and Lancashire Powerboat Racing Club of St Helens. The event was truly International, attracting among the 37 competitors entries from USA, South Africa, France, Germany and Italy, Belgium and Ireland. The race was won in fine style by Roberto Molinari of Italy. But a shadow

BELOW Richard Solomon and family in *Sheba*, Early 1970s

was cast over the event by the accidental death of Bill Shakespeare. During a morning practice run for the race his cat jumped out of the water and sank just south of the clubhouse. Despite frantic efforts the rescue team and divers were unable to save him. The first GP did not enjoy the calmest weather but continued to 1975. The Duke of York GPs were the premier European circuit race and saw the first appearance outside the U.S.A. of the mighty rotary outboards. The Outboard Motor Corporation

(Evinrude and Johnson motors) sent a team of four boats and all their top brass and race engineers, the engines all perished bar one which, driven by Downard and Posey, won. Average speeds increased to 79 mph. It is interesting to compare this with the One Hour record achieved in race conditions by Ted Walsh in Daculina of 77.99 mph in 2001. The GPs would not have lasted an hour and Ted kept going for another 2 hours averaging 70.39 mph.

THE INTRODUCTION OF THE TUNNEL-HULLED CATS CHANGED THE COMPLEXION OF RACING

ABOVE Air entrapment / catamarans racing at Broad Leys, early 1970s

LEFT Air entrapment racing, 1992. Alan Marshall, Chris George and Tim Whitehead.

LADY RACERS

It might be thought that powerboat racing, with its emphasis on speed and engines, was a typically male pursuit. In fact women have often excelled, and still do, in the same way that Amy Johnson and others did in the early days of aviation. Betty Carstairs was the star of powerboat racing in the earliest days of the club. Women racing drivers have been prominent throughout the club's history. A list culled from the club's archives would include Mrs Cooper Pattinson, Miss Willoughby, Lady Craven, Fiona Lady Arran who set a record of 102 mph in 1979/80, Mrs Derek Craven, Marit Morrison, V (Vera) Lydall ,' a sporting lady', is remembered from the 1940s in many photographs. There were three generations of racing Lydalls. In recent years Cynthia Mould, Julia Young who was also the first lady to sit on a formal club committee (racing), Karen Stevenson, Pip Brooks and Helen Loney have added their names to several annual WMBRC trophies.

BELOW Vera Lydall in *Moira*

RECORDS: THE QUEST FOR SHEER SPEED

'LUNATICS OR FOLK-HEROES?.'

'From the earliest development of steam power, enterprising marine designers recognised the advantages of a large inland lake for their experiments, and the local skill of Lakeland boatbuilders was enlisted, sparked off by the enthusiasm of the local gentry, so that throughout the Victorian era the whole district was a forcing ground for new ideas in this sphere.'

George H. Pattinson (grandson of the builder of Broad Leys) in his book The Great Age of Steam on Windermere refers to steam power here, but the same argument had applied to sail, and then to powerboats. Windermere was an ideal forcing ground, in the forefront of boat design, and has seen some significant firsts.

LEFT   Norman H. Buckley in one of the *Miss Windermere* Boats

BELOW Miss Betty Carstairs

At the turn of the century the two champion designers and racers were Herbert Crossley and Alfred Sladen. Crossley's yachts such as Syren and Naiad won so often that people gave up competing with him, reserving their competition for the second place - a problem occasionally familiar in other fields from motorboats to cycling. In the big freeze of 1895 his ice yacht was timed at 38 1/2 mph, the fastest ever achieved on Windermere under sail and a speed not to be equalled by powerboats for many a year. He was rivalled by the Sladen brothers, Alfred and Mortimer. Alfred designed and raced many successful yachts, all built by George Brockbank. His steam launches Phantom, Elphin and Otto (which is preserved) were capable of impressive speeds. His Bat of 1891, also preserved, set a world first when it was worked remotely by radio control in 1904. Osprey was another speedy launch, but was beaten by Williamson's Satanella of 1907 which capable of 40 m.p.h. These early speedboats were long and narrow, with very low freeboard, slicing through the water like Charles Parsons' revolutionary seagoing yacht Turbinia, powered by steam turbines, which caused such a sensation at the Spithead Review of 1897.

BETTY CARSTAIRS

In the late 1920s there was intense rivalry between British drivers and Gar (Garfield) Wood of the United States, who had been setting records in a succession of boats, always named Miss America. He was the first to reach 100 m.p.h. on water, when he managed an average of 92.86 mph. In 1928 Betty Carstairs tested Estelle II on Windermere, then took it, tuned to be capable of 128 mph to The States to wrest the International Trophy from the great rival. But her boat overturned and sank. She and engineer Joe Harris were lucky to escape with broken ribs.

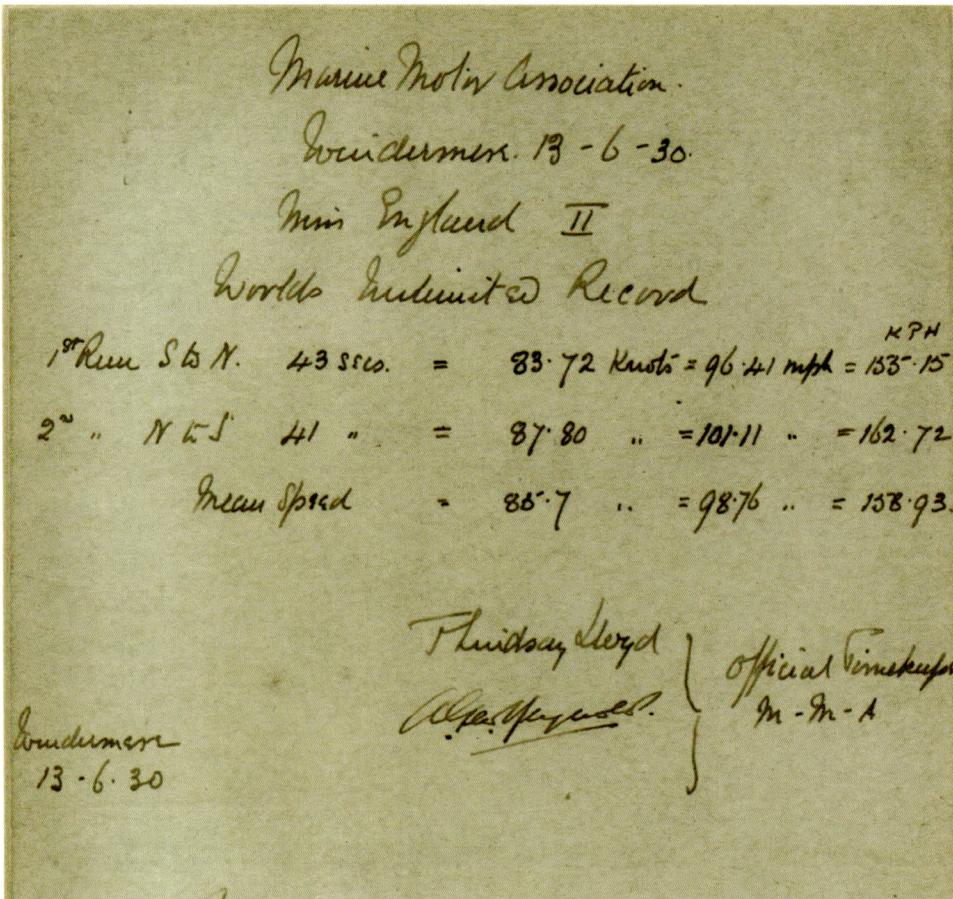

Marine Motor Association.
Windermere. 13 - 6 - 30.
Miss England II
Worlds Unlimited Record

		KPH
1st Run S to N.	43 secs. =	83·72 Knots = 96·41 mph = 155·15
2nd " N to S	41 " =	87·80 " =101·11 " = 162·72
mean Speed	-	85·7 " = 98·76 " = 158·93.

Lindsay Lloyd
Alex Meynell.} Official Timekeeper
M - M - A

Windermere
13 - 6 - 30

LEFT   Certified timing sheet for *Miss England II*

BELOW Sir Henry Segrave

RIGHT   *Miss England II* and Sir Henry Segrave, 1930

SIR HENRY SEGRAVE

Segrave (1896-1930) was the first person to travel at over 200 mph on land, reaching 203 mph in 1927 and 231.45 mph in 1929. In 1930 he set himself to beat the world water speed record as well. Segrave, who had beaten his close friend but arch rival Gar Wood on the water in America in 1929 and was knighted on his return, wanted the new record to be to set here on Windermere. His new boat was Miss England II, built in Cowes and christened here on 5th June 1930. She was big - 38ft 6in overall with a beam of 10ft 6in and weighing over four tons. There were fore and aft rudders, and a single planing step. Twin 1850 hp Rolls Royce aero-engines spun a tiny two-bladed propellor at 12,500 rpm (the gearbox multiplying the revs by 4), producing an immense spray wake at speed. On 13th June, with Michael Willcox ex-RN and Victor Halliwell of Rolls Royce, Segrave set out from the Low Wood to attempt a new record. In perfect conditions Miss England II reached 96.4 mph on the first run, and then 101.11. Although they had reached the 100 m.p.h. target it was not quite enough for a 100 m.p.h. average, so they turned for a third run. This time they may have reached nearly 120 mph but, watched from dozens of small boats and hundreds on shore, the boat started to weave and then lifted and spun out of control, throwing the three men out of the cockpit. The mechanic Halliwell was drowned, Michael Willcocks badly injured though he survived. Segrave was pulled out unconscious, and died in hospital after briefly regaining consciousness. 'Did we do it?' were his last words.

Speed on water is a dangerous business, record attempts doubly so.

ABOVE   Edward Spurr in speedboat *Empire Day*, May 1938

LEFT   Final adjustments for *Empire Day*

BELOW   Heading out in *Empire Day*

(All images courtesy of Windermere Steamboat Museum)

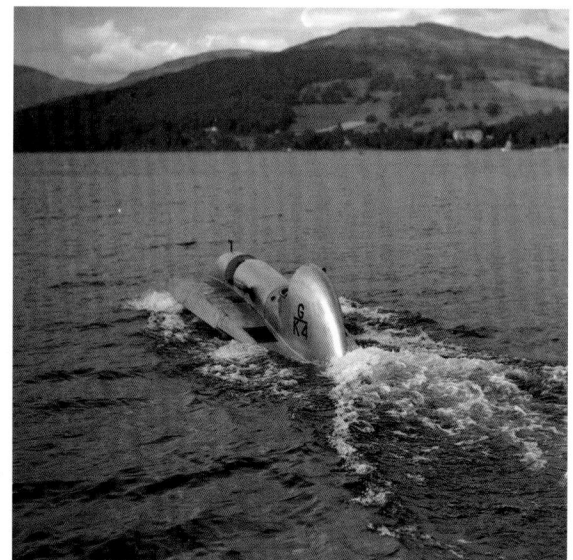

> 'ANY MAN THAT IS GOING TO SUCCEED, AND I DON'T CARE WHAT WALK OF LIFE HE CHOOSES, IS GOING TO HAVE TO BE SELFISH.'
> DONALD CAMPBELL

DONALD CAMPBELL AND BLUEBIRD

Donald Campbell seemed as though compelled to equal, if not surpass, his father's achievements. In the 1930s Malcolm Campbell had held both land and water speed records, achieving 301.335 mph on Bonneville Flats in 1935 and 129.56 mph on Lake Maggiore in 1937, and then 141.740 mph on Coniston in 1939. He died of a stroke in 1948 - one of the few speed record holders of his era to die of natural causes.

'My father was a terrific example, courageous, colourful, dour, unbending, uncompromising.'

Seven months later Donald was in the cockpit of his father's boat Bluebird K4. In 1949 he brought it back to Coniston and had a go at some records, but in 1951 the boat suffered structural failure at 170 mph. With a backing team of Frank Lydall, Norman Buckley, Clem Haworth and others from the club he went up to Loch Ness in October 1952 to assist with John Cobb's world record attempt in his jet speedboat Crusader. Cobb (1899-1952), who had set the land speed record of 394.19mph in a Railton special in 1947, was killed in the attempt at more than 200 mph. Buckley recalled that he was very fatalistic - 'wouldn't go near a lifejacket' - and of very even temperament compared with Campbell.

BELOW Donald Campbell's father Malcolm Campbell

After these two events Campbell decided that he had to develop a new boat. Bluebird K7 was designed by Ken and Lew Norris, an all-metal 3-point hydroplane propelled by a Metropolitan Vickers Beryl jet engine producing 3,500 lbf (16 kN) of thrust. An ugly thing with forward sponsons like a blue lobster, or (more appropriately) a scorpion, quite small but heavy. K7 was unveiled in late 1954, and taken to Ullswater in January 1955 for testing.

The first trials were disappointing. K7 tended to burrow down into the water, refusing to rise up, unstick and plane. By analysis and experiment the weight was redistributed and the configuration of the sponsons adjusted. After much trial and error, Campbell succeeded on 23 July 1955 in setting a new record of 202.15 mph (325.33 km/h). WMBRC members Andrew Brown, Frank Lydall and Norman Buckley were there.

Campbell kept pushing his own record up year by year, achieving 225.63 mph on Coniston in 1956, 239.07 mph in 1957, then 248 mph and finally 260 mph in 1959. 'The boat went mad and I am lucky to have lived through it' he said after a high speed run.

In 1960 he made a fresh attempt at the land speed record with Bluebird-Proteus CN7 at Bonneville Flats, Utah, in the USA, but at 350 mph he crashed, suffering serious injuries. The car was rebuilt for another attempt in 1963 on Lake Eyre, a dried lake bed in Australia. This time rain fell, the first for many years; so much so that CN7 had to be rescued from flood waters. The surface was never as good afterwards, and a further attempt in 1964 was unsuccessful.

Now he returned to the water speed record, achieving 276.33 mph in K7 at Lake Dumbleyung in Australia in 1964. 300 mph was within reach and so, in autumn 1966, Campbell and Bluebird returned to Coniston.

Dawn in winter is the best time to attempt the highest speed on water. Before sunrise the lake is completely still and mirror-like, steely blue but soft-looking. The high fells are crystal clear, glowing pink as they catch the first rays of the sun. It doesn't last. All too soon, as the temperature begins to rise, catspaws appear on the lake and the first innocent clouds blossom on the

'I AM ALWAYS SCARED STIFF WHEN I MAKE A RECORD ATTEMPT'
DONALD CAMPBELL

LEFT   Donald Campbell with Norman H. Buckley and mechanics on K7, July 1955, Ullswater

BELOW   Donald Campbell

RIGHT   Donald Campbell in an early record attempt in *Bluebird*

SPEED ON WATER IS A DANGEROUS
BUSINESS, RECORD ATTEMPTS
DOUBLY SO.

highest peak. The fields are still pearly with frost but pink streaks are reflected in the lake. The mountains, which were so clear, soon disappear behind a sausage of cloud. As the light grows the lake roughens up, and by breakfast time it is too late.

The team, including Norman Buckley and Andrew Brown of WMBRC, with Robin Brown who maintained the electrical systems, assembled at Coniston in November 1966 to attempt the 300 m.p.h. target. The weather seemed set against them, and trials did not go well. Bluebird was now fitted with a Bristol Siddeley Orpheus 701 turbojet developed for the Gnat training plane, as used by the Red Arrows 1964-79, but was still reluctant to plane. There were problems reaching full power, and the air

intakes were damaged.

At last on 4th January 1967 the conditions seemed perfect. The lake was calm and still, the boat fully prepared. After all the delays and frustration, it was now or never. The first leg went well, although at its full speed Bluebird was only marginally stable. Campbell observed a 'Water Barrier' - severe vibration or 'tramping' which set in at 210 - 250 mph. This was visible to observers as a characteristically rhythmic 'rooster tail' spray. The cause of the final crash on the return leg is not fully determined, however Campbell's last words were 'I'm galloping over the top'.

Campbell was killed instantly as Bluebird broke up and sank into deep water, carrying him with it.

NORMAN BUCKLEY AND RECORDS WEEK

Donald Campbell was mercurial, getting the limelight, the press conferences, the posthumous fame. In contrast Norman Buckley, although he broke and/or set eleven world records, was 'shy, bespectacled and self-effacing'. 'I always tried to break my records with as little publicity as possible' he wrote, explaining 'immediately you publicise it you get boats coming and disturbing the water.' He and Campbell took it in turns to attempt records, but where Campbell went for absolute speed Buckley went for endurance.

Buckley did however describe the sensations of absolute speed well. 'When the boat gets over 100 mph. its a funny feeling but you seem to get lifted out of the world. She comes right out of the water, and you seem to be skimming.' 'Over 100 mph. the engine noise seems to disappear' he said, although 'When you come out of a record you're usually a bit deaf, because you've got the exhaust in your ear and it takes about two hours for you to hear properly'.

Norman Buckley was always interested in speed, starting with motorbikes and 'learning to skid around sand which was to help me later on when I came to skid round buoys on Lake Windermere - very similar indeed.' In 1930 he bought and raced a Riley Nine, meanwhile practicing as a solicitor in Manchester. A succession of cars followed, including a 4 1/2 litre Le Mans and an 8 litre Bentley. In 1935 he bought a piece of land in the Winster Valley and built a bungalow for weekends and holidays. Next door lived Derek Craven, son of Sir Charles and keen racing member of the WMBC. In 1939 he decided to move permanently, and through his friend the estate agent (and WMBC Secretary) William McVey he bought Cragwood, next door to Brockhole on Windermere, from Sir John Dodd. Cragwood, now a hotel, is a beautiful Arts and Crafts house of 1910 designed by Frank Dunkerley. A Brough Superior motorbike took him backwards and forwards between Manchester and Windermere.

WHEN THE BOAT GETS OVER 100 MPH. ITS A FUNNY FEELING BUT YOU SEEM TO GET LIFTED OUT OF THE WORLD.

NORMAN BUCKLEY

ABOVE Norman H. Buckley

BELOW Cragwood, home of Norman Buckley, built 1910

LEFT Norman with wife Betty and his mechanic Arthur Henderson

ABOVE *Miss Windermere III*

BELOW Norman H. Buckley and *Miss Windermere IV*

In 1941 he joined the club. His first boat was Miss Windermere II, originally Moonbeam and bought for £700 from Alderman Village. (Miss Windermere I was Derek Craven's boat; he was killed in a car crash in 1945). Miss Windermere II was an American hydroplane powered by a 6-cylinder Lycoming engine and capable of 65 mph. Buckley managed to replace the engine with a rare Jaguar XK120 engine, and in 1950 took three endurance records. All this in considerable pain with his knee, which he had badly damaged a fortnight earlier after a race, 'exceedingly well protected by a large splint with a lot of padding round it'. An additional hazard happened when his petrol tank split and he found the bottom of the boat swilling around with 30 gallons of high octane fuel, 'smelling both sweet and very sinister'.

At the 1951 International, as recounted above, Miss Windermere II was beaten by the Canadian Art Hatch in his three-point 'prop-rider' Costa Living to take the Duke of York trophy. Buckley promptly persuaded Art to sell him the boat, for £300. With Arthur Henderson of Rochdale, his faithful mechanic (and brother in law), he replaced the V8 Mercury engine with a Jaguar XK120 C-type, redesigning the streamlined cowling to fit. He was now racing at 90 mph and, with the engine converted to D-type took a new 89 mph endurance record.

Miss Windermere IV, a sturdier boat, was built here in Bowness by Borwicks. Buckley and Miss Windermere IV set four new records, using three different engines. Miss Windermere IV is preserved in the Steamboat Museum. A varnished mahogany hull shaped like a flying saucer, or a horseshoe crab to be more accurate, fitted with an inboard Jaguar

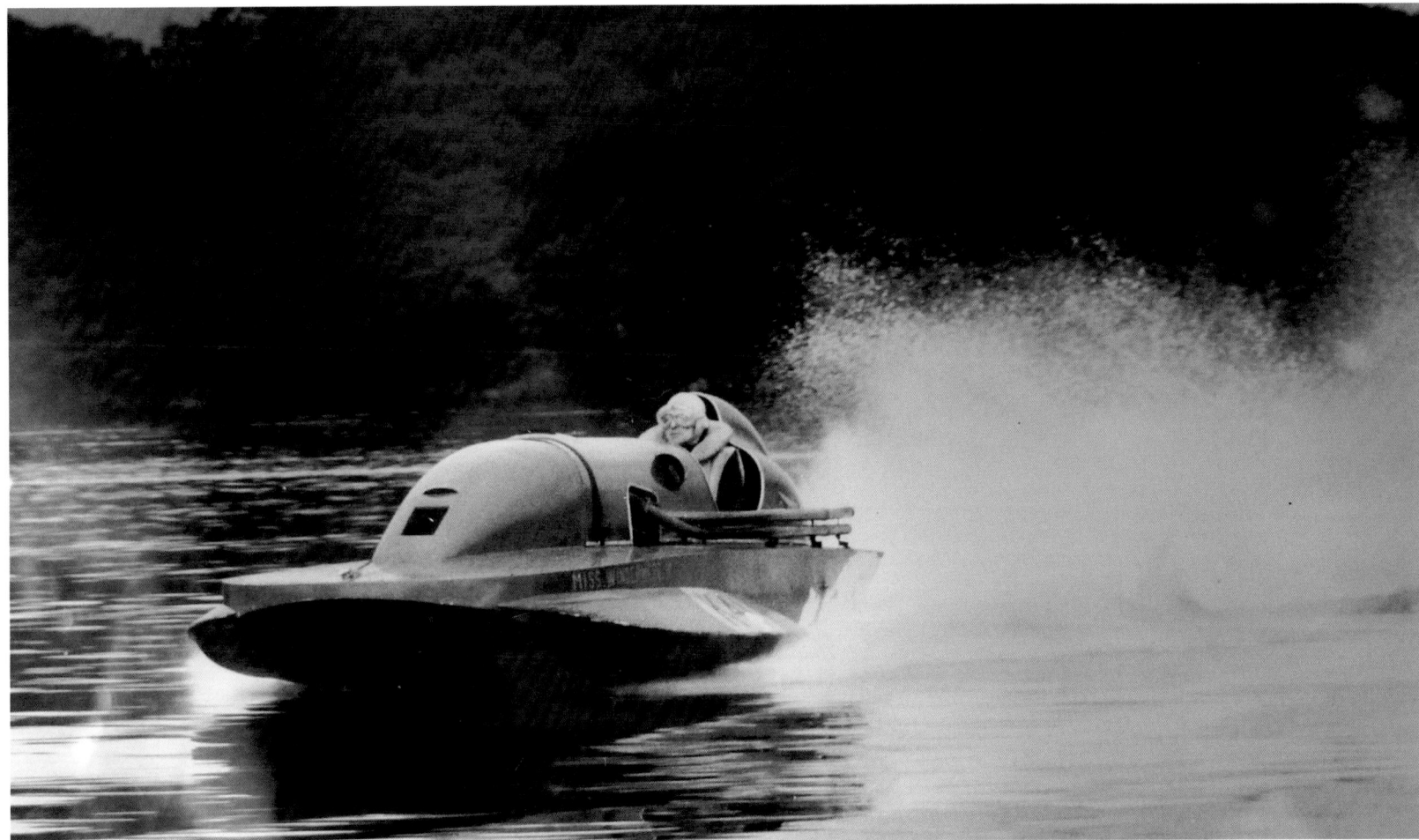

engine and steering wheel. Engine and rear cockpit are housed in a red nacelle with a stubby tailfin.

Donald Campbell's death in 1967 shook him badly. Norman Buckley had been the timekeeper as usual. He decided to give up motorboating completely, saying 'Its time to quit now. When you're getting up in your sixties is time to forget about it.' He had got interested in the hotel business, buying the Lowwood in 1952, the Wild Boar in 1959, the Royal in Bowness in 1965, and then Langdale Chase. However that did not stop him, aged 64, taking Miss Windermere IV out during the first Records Week and taking a National immersed prop record of 113.7 mph.

Tony Fahey negotiated with Norman Buckley to drive his Miss Windermere V, with a highly modified Jaguar V12 engine. On 22 May 1977 Fahey set two World and one National speed records, with one run of over 154 mph. Miss Windermere V was later named Vladivar.

Records Week was the brainchild of Norman Buckley. In 1971, the same year as the International Grand Prix (see above), he had the idea and the initiative for an annual Records Week, when records of all sorts could be set up and broken. It was to take place on Windermere opposite The Low Wood, one of his five hotels, at the end of October. In those days most of the hotels shut for winter, and the event added a week to their season. The initial sponsors were BP, and entrants were allowed to compete only on one day, but could make more than one attempt on that day. Nicholas Huddleston in Septimus and Richard Solomon in Sheba were among several club members who achieved national records during the ealy Record Weeks. BP's sponsorship had set the event on a sound footing, but other sponsors needed to be found for 1975 and 1976. In 1977 the agreed

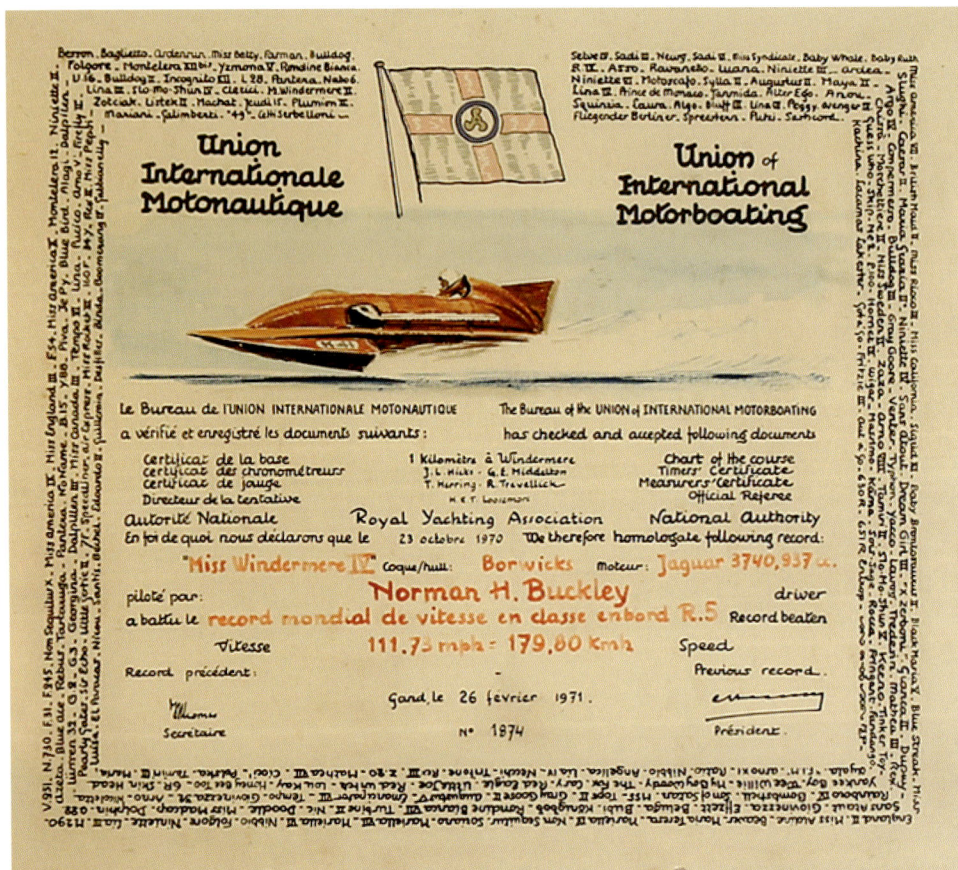

BELOW *Miss Windermere IV* today at Windermere Steamboat Museum

LEFT Certificate of speed for Norman H. Buckley and *Miss Windermere IV, 1971*

ABOVE Norman H. Buckley and his team in *Miss Windermere IV*

sponsors pulled out late in the day, in August, and Records Week had to be cancelled.

This was a blow, but from 1978, determined that it should not happen again, the officials and entrants have borne their own expenses, with a subsidy from Norman Buckley's chain of hotels. 19 world and 150 national records had been set by then. The committee now involves enthusiasts from all over the country, and the event has continued ever since,

under the WMBRC flag, though as we shall see later, since 2005 transferred to Coniston.

When Norman Buckley died suddenly in 1974 he had started to gather material for an autobiography, to be written by Kevin Desmond. It was never completed. He left Miss Windermere V to Tony Fahey, though this was subsequently wrecked.

LADY ARRAN

'An elegantly spoken lady, very photogenic'. In 1972 Fiona, Lady Arran, brought Highland Fling, designed for her by Lorne Campbell of Vosper, to Windermere to compete in the world championships. She took the class 1 record at 82 mph, which caused some controversy because Highland Fling was class 2 boat, with just one Mercury outboard. Highland Fling was apparently horrible to race, because although fast in a straight line she was extremely difficult to turn. In 1972 she and her navigator, Robert Trigg, took the class 2 world record on Windermere in Skean Dhu at 92 mph.

Having got this close she decided in 1980 to have a go at the ton - 100 mph. The attempt was not without incident. Skean Dhu (=little dagger) arrived with a bang, demolishing the club's gateposts and waking everyone in the lodge. Then, on trial, it blew its engine. The new engine when it arrived had to be run in, so the boat trundled up and down at slow speeds in front of the clubhouse with Lady Arran driving with various young members of the White and Mould families on board, all of whom eventually became racing drivers at WMBRC.

On the first attempt Lady Arran achieved 99.5 mph. The next day she managed 106 mph on the first run, 98 on the return, which gave her an average of 102 mph. She was the first woman in the world to travel at more than 100 mph on water.

Lady Arran was then 62, and having achieved her aim decided to retire from power boats. Not for an easy retirement however, but to take up the demanding sport of horse driving.

She sadly died in May 2013 at the grand age of 94 years.

ABOVE   Ready to Go: Norman Buckley examines the controls of *Miss Windermere IV* (Courtesy of Windermere Steamboat Museum)

BELOW   Lady Arran

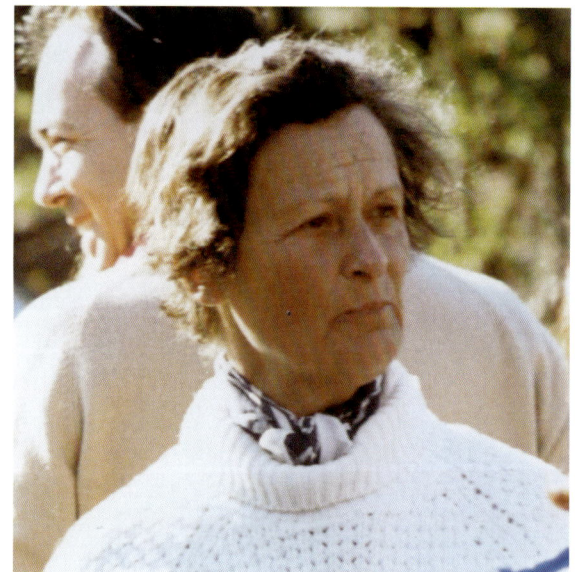

THE FASTEST GRANNY ON WATER

RECORDS WEEK ON CONISTON 2011-2012

'One thing seems certain, racing members of the Windermere Motor Boat Racing Club will attempt to win new records and will help others to do so as long as attempts are made.' This was the last sentence of the 1975 history of the WMBRC. When the 10 mph speed limit came in on Windermere the inspector recommended that an exception could be made for Records Week to continue at the Low Wood. The Lake District National Park Authority (LDNPA) said no. So the WMBRC said OK, Coniston it is. You must be joking was the LDNPA response. The Club said read the Coniston by-laws; world and national record attempts are permitted. Besides, the memory of Donald Campbell lingers strong. So Records Week is still held every year on Coniston at the end of the season, now in early November. It is the only high speed powerboating event still held in the Lake District, and draws big

BELOW U11 Unlimited *Namonai* 178mph
(All Record Week images courtesy of Malcolm Casson Photography)

crowds. In fact Coniston as a venue is better than the Lowwood for competitors and spectators, as well as having the Bluebird cachet.

What is needed for record attempts is a big enough stretch of water to get the clear measured kilometre at full speed in the middle. Records can be claimed in many different categories. Inboard / outboard. Ladies / gents. Capacity / type of fuel / weight of boat. Even power source - there are records for electric and steam boats.

The **41st Records Week in 2011** was heralded by dire weather forecasts, which discouraged some of the hydroplanes and fast cats from attending. Two events involving WMBRC drivers stand out. One was the appearance of the replica Bluebird K777 (built in Lytham by WMBRC members the Morris family and Helical Technology) with Past Commodore of WMBRC Jim Noone in the cockpit. As Donald Campbell had discovered, getting the boat to rise up and plane across the water proved difficult. The first attempts led to ignominious swamping, and it was only on the second day that something like its true performance was revealed. The other event was more dramatic. Pip Brooks in her bright magenta cat managed an average of 97 mph but her attempt to break the 100 mph barrier was foiled by a sudden gust of wind which sent her craft into an aerial loop-de-loop. Luckily she was picked up quickly and almost unhurt, though shaken. The boat however was a write-off.

BELOW Unlimited prototype electric, Peter White N 32.7mph

Many other WMBRC present day and past drivers have established National records in their various classes (See App 1). Jim Noone in Miss Windermere VI, built by Peter Lee, and Donald Campbell in Bluebird are, until now, the only holders of the K7 platinum star - over 150mph.

Records Week 2012 opened with ideal weather conditions: clear, bright and still. Eight world records tumbled on that first day. A speed of 176.1 mph was set by John William Myers in a huge lime-green American hydroplane. An impressive sight on the lake, sending up sheets of spray, especially at the corners. An impressive sight on its trailer too, making

an unlikely companion to the sedate steam-powered Gondola, out of the water for the winter. High drama ensued too, when Chris Loney WMBRC flipped his Dac. The boat somersaulted twice - and landed him the right way up, and dry! Luckily he came out unhurt and was soon on the water again. Later in the week the weather predictably deteriorated but records were attempted and broken over the spectrum of powerboating, from tiny jetskis to huge twin-engined seagoing boats. Peter White of WMBRC set a new National Record in a prototype all-aluminium electric boat to join Helen Loney as the only two holders of electric boat records.

ABOVE Vieser / Selva Club 1000
Peter Hart N 57.81mph

BELOW Ted Walsh trying to add to his many World and National records. DAC / Mercury

ABOVE R2 RIB Mannerfelt,
Peter Hart N 77.63mph

LEFT Unlimited Monno Clubman,
Chris Loney N 81.22mph

BLUEBIRD UPDATE

ABOVE Trial of *Bluebird replica K777*, on at Coniston Record Week, 2011

BELOW Jim Noone in *Bluebird replica K777*

K7, the original craft salvaged from the bottom of the lake, is being slowly and painstakingly restored at North Shields, preserving every possible scrap of the original. Every crumpled component is ironed out like a Tunnock's Teacake wrapper. Even the bits that cannot be used go in the LOF (Loss of Original Fabric) box to be melted down for rivets. The engine casing was Magnesium, which has preserved the rest by quietly fizzing away as a sacrificial anode, so the engine didn't suffer internal corrosion. The restoration has posed some interesting debates. The wiring, for instance, was primitive (like most British machines of that date), and the fuel system not much better.

The K777 was built by the Morris family, members of WMBRC and owners of Helical Technology. The family were inspired to build the K777 by the heroic achievements of Donald Campbell in breaking both the land and water speed records and ensuring that he remained an iconic symbol of British achievements showing remarkable personal courage, perseverance and determination in his quest for world records using leading edge British engineering and design.

Externally, K777 is very similar to that of Bluebird K7 in her last configuration. However, internally she is very different in that K777 has been built using the most modern and advanced engineering techniques. For instance she has an internal space frame made of seamless square aluminium alloy tube, and is fitted with a UIM registered cockpit safety cell made of carbon fibre and is 500lbs lighter than Bluebird K7.

She is 26 ft 4" in length, with a 10 ft x 6 ft beam at the sponsons, has a jet fighter plane Folland Gnat vertical tail mounted on top of the cowling at the rear, and is powered by a Bristol Siddeley Orpheus turbojet capable of producing 4520lbf of thrust . K777 made her first public appearance while she was being transported to Coniston Water in the Lake District for her first water trials at the Powerboat Records Week 2011. After similar problems to Campbell's first attempt to get the craft on the plane she successfully completed several speed runs, culminating with a brief three point planing run with experienced power boat driver and a delighted enthusiast Jim Noone at the helm.

WMBRC AT BARROW

'THE THING ABOUT MOTORBOAT RACING IS THAT YOU HAVE TO KEEP IT ALL GOING - NOT JUST THE BOATS, BUT ENGINEERING AND EXPERIMENTATION, DRIVING SKILLS, THE SAFETY TEAM AND EQUIPMENT, AND THE TIMING EXPERTISE.'

THE SPEED LIMIT

There was always bound to be conflict between those who love the excitement of speed and power and those who value the Lakes for their peace and tranquillity. The first major row was as long ago as 1911; not, curiously enough, over a boat but over 'a beastly fly-swimming spluttering aeroplane careering up and down Windermere'. The story is recounted earlier.

As speeds increased so resistance to powerboating on Windermere gathered strength, but the speed limit was a long time coming. Here's the run up to the ban:

Letters of complaint about motorboats are a recurring feature from the 1920s, as the club's archives prove. Harold Pattinson was generally deputed to answer them. Miss Carstairs in particular was a popular figure when she raced on Windermere, helping to neutralise opposition to motorboat racing and record attempts. There was a flurry of complaints in 1960. More came in 1975, and again in 1991-4. The club accused the National Park of being confrontational on the issue in 1994, while accepting the need to implement a sensible management plan to cope with motorboats. In general it was not the dozen or so organised race days in the year that caused maximum irritation, but the unregulated proliferation of water-skiing and jet-skis.

As boats became faster and the lake more crowded there was concern over increasing incidents. Although WMBRC's own safety record is good there was clearly a perceived problem by the LDNPA. In 1992 the LDNPA put proposals to the Home Office to restrict speed. It was supported by conservation organisations and the South Lakeland District Council, but opposed by the WMBRC, by powerboaters and water skiers, and by a significant proportion of the business community.
The Home Secretary ordered an enquiry.
In 1994 the Enquiry began. Its report was presented to Secretary of State for the Environment in 1996, recommending that the limit be confirmed.
But the then Secretary of State disagreed, refusing to confirm the order on the grounds that Windermere was a public highway and an important power-boating venue - indeed the only inland one.
The LDNPA then applied for a Judicial Review. This was granted in November 1996.
A General Election followed.
The new Government reviewed the original 1996 findings, and confirmed them.
And finally, the speed limit on Windermere of 10

LEFT 2005, the last day of racing at Broad Leys before the speed limit. Racing drivers, safety patrol, officers of the day and timing pier officials gather for a photo call

nautical miles per hour (10 knots) was set to come into force in March 2005.

High speed motor boat racing on Windermere, the very reason for the club's existence, was no longer possible. Motor boat racing is built into the club's title - but then so is Windermere. The two are now severed.

Three last race days on Windermere were run at the club in quick succession, the final one being on Easter Monday 2005. Many members and friends turned up to watch some great racing and enjoy the unique social atmosphere of a drink on the clubhouse terrace afterwards. The day ended memorably but with great sadness as after 80 years of racing on Windermere the club had to find a new venue but would contine to put forward a case to return in the future.

Of course, like any well run organisation the club had seen the ban coming. Steps had already been taken both to move the high speed events elsewhere, and to diversify activities on the lake and at Broad Leys. The WMBRC committee delegated Peter White and Ted Walsh to investigate alternative stretches of water for racing. Cropper's reservoir at the head of Kentmere was just big enough, but hopeless for access. Pine Lakes near the M6 was assessed, and Killington Lake. A freshwater pit outside Barrow was ruled out for its sheer edges. The best candidate was Barrow docks, and an agreement was reached with Associated British Ports to make a trial of racing in Ramsden Dock. As it turned out the 2003 All Classes National at Barrow was particularly successful. The sun shone, Barrow was delighted, the crowd loved it.

'IN 2025 THE CLUB WILL SURELY ACHIEVE ITS CENTENARY OF MOTOR BOAT RACING ON WINDERMERE'

WMBRC BOOK (1975)
50 YEARS OF MOTOR BOAT RACING).

RAMSDEN DOCK RACING

The layout at Ramsden Dock is ideal for setting an inshore racing course which would also allow WMBRC to hold club, national and possibly international events. Also the Barrow weather is consistently better than that at Windermere, because the clouds tend to go straight over. In any case racing in the enclosed dock can usually continue even in bad weather, unlike Windermere where wind and swell can prevent racing.

At the same time as the speed restriction had been imposed on Windermere, Barrow Council had been allocated a £52m development grant to transform the working dock into a modern marina with 400 berths, with hotels and restaurants on the dockside and a major water sport centre. As part of this strategic plan the council was keen to embrace powerboat racing, which was seen as having the most potential

to attract spectators.

Unfortunately not much of the grand plan has come to fruition as yet, apart from a partially-built promenade and some site clearance.

Looking for diversification and fresh attractions in the town, Barrow Council asked the WMBRC to participate in their first Festival of the Sea, to be held in June 2006. 'A Funfair, F1 simulator, surf machine simulator, a rodeo bull, Asian cookery display, Punch and Judy, face painting, BMX and skateboard demonstrations, and antique buses' were all promised - plus a National Power boating event in Ramsden Dock including Formula 2 catamarans, hydoplanes and clubman class. WMBRC members participated in several events. Two warships and a historic tall ship the Jacinta would be in attendance and, most excitingly, there would be a chance to see inside

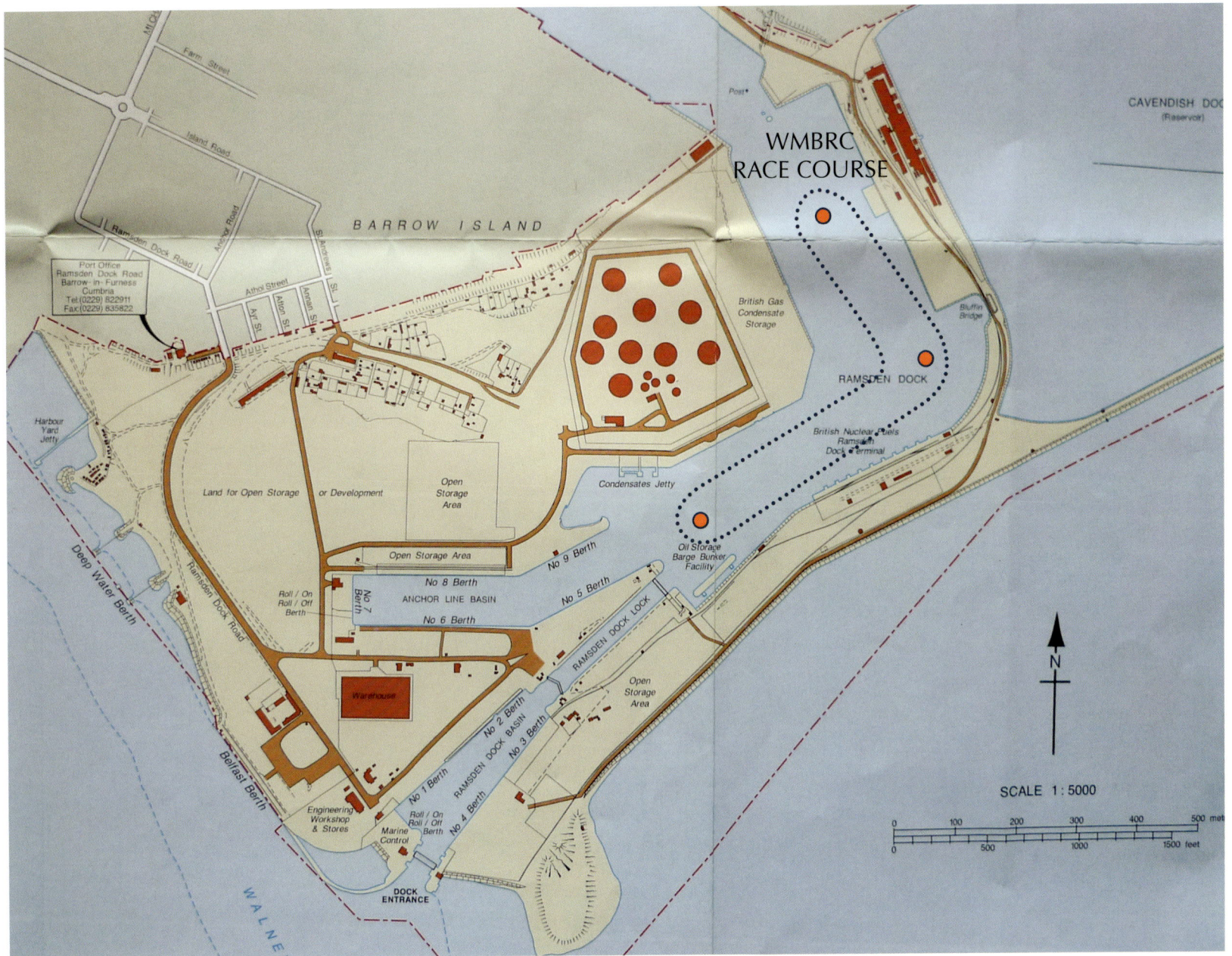

Map labels:

CAVENDISH DOCK (Reservoir)

WMBRC RACE COURSE

BARROW ISLAND

Farm Street
Island Road
Ramsden Dock Road
Anchor Road
St Andrews St
Athol Street
Annan St
Ayr St
Afton St

Port Office
Ramsden Dock Road
Barrow-in-Furness
Cumbria
Tel (0229) 822911
Fax (0229) 835822

British Gas Condensate Storage

Bluffin Bridge

RAMSDEN DOCK

British Nuclear Fuels Ramsden Dock Terminal

Condensates Jetty

Harbour Yard Jetty

Oil Storage Barge Bunker Facility

Land for Open Storage or Development

Open Storage Area

Open Storage Area

No 9 Berth

No 8 Berth   ANCHOR LINE BASIN

No 5 Berth

No 7 Berth

No 6 Berth

Roll / On Roll / Off Berth

Warehouse

RAMSDEN DOCK LOCK

Open Storage Area

Deep Water Berth

Ramsden Dock Road

Belfast Berth

No 2 Berth   RAMSDEN DOCK BASIN

No 3 Berth

No 1 Berth

No 4 Berth

Engineering Workshop & Stores

Marine Control

Roll / On Roll / Off Berth

DOCK ENTRANCE

WALNEY

N

SCALE 1 : 5000

0   100   200   300   400   500 met
0   500   1000   1500 feet

ABOVE Plan of Ramsden Dock in Barrow
showing the race course

DDH - the giant shed of Devonshire Dock Hall where nuclear submarines are constructed. The festival was a hugely ambitious event. However, numbers attending were never quite as great as anticipated, the grant was progressively cut, DDH was taken out of the recipe 'for health and safety reasons', and after a few years the Barrow Festival of the Sea fizzled out.

However, powerboat racing at Barrow is now an established fact. It is a long drive. Barrow is a notoriously long way from anywhere, especially with a boat on a trailer. So Saturday race days start early, especially for the supporting staff. Several members will arrive early enough to enjoy an 8.30 breakfast at the local dockside supermarket.

The race venue is an exposed L-shaped peninsula bounded one one side by Ramsden Dock and on the other by the brackish waters of Cavendish Dock, now used to cool Roosecote Power Station. A place of windblown scrub and industrial litter. Looming over the scene are three disarmed naval corvettes, sleek, grey and pointless. They were ordered in 1995

AS SPEEDS HAVE INCREASED, SO SAFETY REGULATIONS - NEGLIGIBLE IN THE EARLY DAYS - HAVE HAD TO BE TIGHTENED

by the Royal Navy of Brunei, a tiny but oil-rich Sultanate on the coast of Borneo, paid for, but never delivered. Built in Scotstoun, Glasgow, and launched in 2001 and 2002.

Also tied up in Ramsden Dock are Pacific Heron, Pacific Egret and Pacific Grebe, smart blue and white ships with PTNL emblazoned on the funnel. These were built in 2007/8 and 2010 for transporting spent nuclear fuel, vitrified waste, mixed oxide fuel, and plutonium between Barrow and Japan. The Fukushima disaster in March 2011 has put their future in doubt.

So the backdrop to racing is somewhat different from wooded lakeside and gracious villas and boathouses of Windermere, consisting of the two groups of parked high tech ships and the gas tanks on the far side of Ramsden Dock. Away to the north is the red stone clocktower of Barrow Town Hall and, if you are lucky, a glimpse of the southwestern fells. Over the mudflats to the south is Piel Castle on its islet, an amazing landmark visible for miles across Morecambe Bay. Mainland Lancashire may be seen too, with the twin lumps of Heysham power station and even, thirty miles away, Blackpool tower. Out at sea is the largest wind farm in Europe.

One of the club's officials has to sign in with the harbourmaster on duty before any activity can take place in the dock. Any movement of shipping means that racing has to stand down for a while. Luckily plenty of time is given for major movements, such as when one of the nuclear submarines puts to sea, which would mean no racing at all that day. This in fact happened on 15 September 2012, the penultimate race day of the year.

ABOVE Matthew Wood in *Nauti Bouy*
BELOW Taking the lead, Ted Walsh
(All Barrow racing images courtesy of Malcolm Casson Photography)

THE CREWS OF ALL THE SUPPORT VEHICLES ARE THE UNSUNG HEROES OF POWERBOAT RACING

The Rescue and Patrol teams set out the courses with large orange buoys. The long course is L-shaped, the short course. is triangular . There are usually five or six races, short or long course, during the day.

Racing, which takes place under RYA national circuit rules, cannot start unless there is an ambulance on shore with two or three paramedics at the ready and a specialized rescue craft on the water with a trained diver at the ready in case of an accident. The crews of all the support vehicles are the unsung heroes of powerboat racing. Osprey, a volunteer club founded in the 1980s by the Staffordshire Sub Aqua Club, are at the forefront of international racing safety but the WMBRC will also provide patrol and rescue

crews crews from club members who are trained to emulate the Osprey service as far as possible. The WMBRC rescue boat is fitted with a drop front so that a casualty can be floated head first into the boat. The first few minutes after an accident are vital, so examination and stabilization can take place straight away, while the boat makes its way to the shore. As speeds have increased, so safety regulations - negligible in the early days - have been tightened. Water is an unforgiving element when combined with speed, and life jackets and crash helmets are compulsory. The shock of cold water when the driver is already under stress is an additional hazard. The fastest boats are fitted with a reinforced cockpit and oxygen/air to breathe, and drivers are trained with a

BELOW Alan Marshall in a 2000 Cat

'dunk test' to ensure that they know how to get out quickly.

An upmarket butty van is always available on race days at Barrow. A little different from when racing took place at the Club, when racing paused whilst afternoon tea was served in the club. However needs must, and an offering of a good range of sustenance for participants and spectators in all weathers is much appreciated. The Club has purchased three caravans which serve as toilets and changing facilities, shelter in bad weather, and race control.

All participating race boats must undergo an official scrutinizing before every race day to make sure boat and equipment meet the required RYA standard. All participants will have signed the official RYA form for insurance purposes, and before each race the drivers are briefed by the officer of the day, underlining safety procedures and being given their individual start times.

Racing starts at around 1.30. Boats are handicapped according to their speed expressed in time to complete one lap of the circuit. This is determined

ABOVE Philip Fairhurst in *Rainbow Dancer*
BELOW Paul Brooks in the lead

THE ENCLOSED COURSE AT BARROW IS VERY EXCITING

RIGHT   As close as it gets

BELOW   Ben & Charles Morris in *"The Battleship"*

by the skill of the driver as well as the type of boat. Drivers may range from Peter White, still racing at 72 after having raced every year since 1975, to Matthew Wood who at 21 is currently the youngest driver. The mix of boats in recent years has ranged from 120 m.p.h. Formula 1 cats to single seater monohulls capable of 60 m.p.h. Minimum racing speed is 53 m.p.h. The cats are much faster and scoot round the corners on an even keel. The monohulls are perhaps more exciting to watch because they bank into the corners, with lots of spray, and then accelerate two-thirds out of the water. They are also less impersonal because you can see the crew. On a good day as many as ten boats may start, although breakdowns, bumps and blow-ups are common and can cause some to drop out.

In Barrow, because there are not likely to be other boats on the water, the patrol boats are not needed. Nevertheless two or three safety boats are on the water in case of a breakdown, which is indicated by a yellow flag. A red flag indicates a driver in the water, and everyone stops immediately.

Races are run according to a sophisticated timing system developed by club member and racing driver Ted Walsh. As speeds have increased so timing has had to become more refined and accurate. The analogue system was accurate to only a second, which was not good enough. Race timing went digital in about 2001. The latest mechanism, is accurate to three decimal places, and the timing display, mounted on a caravan, counts down to the start time at zero and then back up again.

There is a designated milling area far enough away from the start line to allow boats to get up to racing speed before they cross the start line at their allotted time. The slowest boat starts first, usually five seconds after the start time. Others follow according to their handicap time, so the fastest starts last. Lots of noise and blue smoke. Unfortunately the parked corvettes,

BELOW Will Getty in *No Guts No Glory* being chased

RIGHT Peter White in *Au-Dela* just ahead

while providing an unusual backdrop, do limit the viewing for spectators, but from a racing driver's point of view the enclosed course at Barrow is very exciting, zooming past the nuclear waste ships on one leg and the warships on the other. In a five lap race the fastest boat may have to lap the slowest twice, which makes for an exciting spectacle when you understand the system. Handicapping is so designed that, in theory, all the participants will finish together. It doesn't happen very often, but makes a fine spectacle when it does.

Racing finishes at around 4.30 or 5 o'clock. The Officer of Duty tots up the points. Drivers and support staff recover their boats from the water, hosing them down and flushing engines with fresh water - salt is bad for craft and for their engines. Buoys are recovered and are stowed away, with the patrol boats, in the brick building on the quayside that Barrow Council allows WMBRC to use free of charge.

Trophies and points are awarded for each race. Even in bad weather the drivers' presentation takes place and a day prize is awarded for maximum points. Trophies are awarded at the Prize Giving dinner at the end of the season. If it is a Flag Officer's day the driver will know he has won that sought-after prize

and drivers and spectators are treated to some nibbles and a drink supplied by the Flag Officer before they leave for home.

Every year around 10 race days are planned in the calendar. With approximately five races per race day a year that means as many as 50+ trophies are available to the drivers on which to have their name inscribed, and share the accolade of winning with some very famous names from the past.

Now the solace for driving back to the clubhouse for a shower and a cocktail, and perhaps dinner, in the beautiful surroundings of Broad Leys, the heart of our powerboat racing fraternity. Drivers are allowed to take the cups they have won to display at home if they wish but most are left with the club and make a really splendid show in the magnificent Broad Leys hall, still the heart of circuit powerboat racing, and where after each race day divers and members are treated on their return from Barrow with fine fare and on several occasions a Disco.

ABOVE   Will Wood in the air

BELOW   Prize giving dinner.
         From left to right: Chris Loney, Will Getty, Matthew Wood, Peter White, Adam Brown, Pip Brooks, Ted Walsh, Alan Marshall, Paul Brooks, Peter Hart, Will Wood, Jim Noone

ABOVE Jim Noone in *Airtours* ahead of the pack

RIGHT Lady racer Pip Brooks keeping ahead

BROAD LEYS: THE HOUSE AND THE CLUB TODAY

FOR ANY CLUB TO SUCCEED, IT REQUIRES THREE ESSENTIAL INGREDIENTS. FIRST, IT SHOULD HAVE THE BENEFITS OF A BEAUTIFUL CLUBHOUSE IN A BEAUTIFUL LOCATION. SECOND, IT SHOULD SERVE GOOD FOOD AND WINE TO KEEP THE MEMBERS HAPPY AND CONTENT AND LAST AND NOT LEAST, IT MUST HAVE THE SUPPORT OF ITS MEMBERS.

LEFT   Sailing at Broad Leys

BELOW   The clubhouse main entrance at Broad Leys

Some may question the link in this book between WMBRC history and one of CFA Voysey's finest houses Broad Leys. However when you quiz Peter White, who had been chairman of House since the late 80s, the importance of this unusual relationship becomes clear.

Not only have there been members and Committees of WMBRC that have appreciated the importance of the house, but they have been prepared to invest heavily in its upkeep and infra structure. They have at all times taken great cognisance of Voysey and the Arts and Crafts style in whatever modifications that have had to take place in order to accommodate the commercial requirements of a Private Members club.

It is estimated that the Club has invested since the 80s almost £750,000 in capital projects in the house and grounds and now annually spend over £140,000 per annum on running and maintaining Broad Leys. To help fund some of the investments, the clubhouse is available to non members for weddings, corporate events and Bed & Breakfast during the week and for a limited number of weekends during the year. This facility has been enjoyed by many Arts and Crafts enthusiasts from all over the world, as well as many brides and grooms who return regularly to celebrate their anniversaries.

The WMBRC today is one of only five speedboat racing clubs in the country. It may also be one of the oldest, together with the Oulton Broad Club. The club flourishes, in spite of the Windermere speed limit, with a strong social scene involving all ages, and varied boating activities at the Club, at Coniston during Records Week, and at Barrow.

There is still plenty of controversy about the speed limit. 'In the best of all worlds racing would come back to Windermere, however, it will hopefully regain some race days on the lake, but inevitably must retain its race days at Barrow. High speed racing is a demanding sport: 'The thing about motorboat racing is that you have to keep it all going - not just the boats, but engineering and experimentation, driving skills, the safety team and equipment, and the timing expertise.'

Although the club was granted two racing days on Windermere in 2013, with a hope that this will be permanent, it seems likely that the club will have to continue to change and diversify in order to keep competitive racing of some sort alive. It is interesting in this context to note that both the National Park and the National Trust are moving towards encouraging more active and challenging activities in the great outdoors.

The Commodore's report for 2012/13 concludes 'For any club to succeed, it requires three essential ingredients. First, it should have the benefits of a beautiful clubhouse in a beautiful location. Second, it should serve good food and wine to keep the members happy and content and last and not least, it must have the support of its members.'
In the end, the key to the club's future may be Broad Leys itself. The house has been celebrated ever since it was built; a prime example of domestic architecture from the time when the art of living reached an all-time high. With its superb position and shoreline, the house deserves its fame.

'IN 2025 THE CLUB WILL SURELY ACHIEVE ITS CENTENARY OF MOTOR BOAT RACING ON WINDERMERE'

WMBRC BOOK (1975)
50 YEARS OF MOTOR BOAT RACING).

SAILING

Although power boat racing is still at the heart of WMBRC, over the years the Club has successfully developed several other Lake based activities

The introduction of competitive sailing events from Broad Leys foreshore has proved to be a very positive development introducing new members and a new water based sport. Dinghy sailing, for which Past Commodore George Lewthwaite gave a cup, was introduced in the early 1980s. The cup was later diverted for Family Week, but is now once again the key sailing trophy.

The core of the WMBRC's sailing programme are the Bénéteau First 21.7 boats. The advantage of a one-class race is that, in theory, all are equal and no handicaps are necessary.

The Bénéteau is a French boat, built by a firm established in Vendée in 1884 which now specialises in volume production of modern fibreglass yachts. Most of their craft are for ocean sailing, and much bigger. The 21.7 is the smallest of their four standard classes, at 7.9 m or nearly 26 feet long, with a small cabin. They are dual purpose boats, quite stubby looking, with a straight stem, wide stern, twin rudders, and tall and narrow high aspect ratio sails. Materials of the hull, mast, rigging and sails are visibly high-tech.

LEFT A return to racing on Windermere in 2013 *(Image courtesy of Malcolm Casson Photography)*

BELOW WMBRC sailing regatta at Broad Leys

Nine or ten sailing race days a year are held, between May and September and timed not to clash with powerboat events. They take place on Windermere, in front of the club, using the club's jetties and timing pier and enjoying the club's setting, ambience and facilities.

The competing boats must be in the water and ready to race at eleven o'clock. The start is signalled from the timing pier by a countdown of flags and hooters. Although most of the competitors belong to the same class, built to the same design, the expertise of their crews varies considerably, so there is a handicapping system after all. Nevertheless the competitors start together over the line, unlike the powerboats which start according to their handicap in order to finish together. It means that the first to finish is not necessarily the winner, which is always confusing to spectators. The sailing course is marked out with buoys, and the number of laps is determined by the officials according to the weather so that each race takes roughly an hour. Windermere can be a tricky and unpredictable place to sail, with sudden squalls and calms. What starts out as a calm sort of day can worsen rapidly, with sudden terrifying gusts which can almost flatten even a reefed boat. Or of course it can go the other way, a good breeze can die down leaving boats becalmed.

Since sailing was introduced by Peter White and Harry Leung buying the first Bénéteau in 2005 the fleet has grown to 14 class boats and now represents the largest Bénéteau Club fleet on the lake Sailing has developed to the point where annual trophies are awarded. Nothing like the number for powerboating, but they are 70 years behind.

During the last 10 years WMBRC have jointly hosted with Maiden Marine both the Bénéteau 21 Regatta in May and the Big Bénéteau Regatta in August. The latter has now grown to the largest Bénéteau Regatta in the UK

BELOW Big Beneteau Regatta at Broad Leys

CLASSIC BOATS

RIGHT Classic Boat Rally, classic boats line up at the
Broad Leys jetties

BELOW A Classic ChrisCraft at the Classic Boat Rally

The British Classic Motor Boat Rally (BCMBR) was founded in the late 1980s by Graham Loney and David Taylor, enthusiasts for the restoration of vintage Riva and Chris Craft boats. Aware that there was no organisation in Britain to foster a gathering of classic mahogany type speedboats, they got in touch first with the Windermere Steamboat Museum at Bowness. The initial response was good, and the museum suggested the WMBRC as another player. It took two years to get it together, and the first rally was held on Windermere in 1990, held partly at the museum and partly at the club. Twenty boats attended from all over the country, which concluded with a speed trial on the Sunday.

With the temporary closure of the Steamboat Museum the WMBRC has hosted the event ever since, extending temporary membership to those attending. It takes place at the end of July or early August. An average of 45 or 50 boats have attended, including several from abroad. These are not flying machines like today's F1 cats, but classic (pre-1970) and classy speedboats designed to do 30-40 mph.

Riva, ChrisCraft, Delta, Simmonds, Healey, Fairey, Broom, Dowty, Jetstar, Century, Poncelet, Albatross.

The year 2004 was the last year of unrestricted motorboat racing on Windermere, and the 'last blast' rally was a major event. 100 boats, including twelve Rivas, came for the best part of a week. Numbers were such that a marquee was set up on the croquet lawn, and 250 sat down for dinner.

The imposition of the speed limit could have spelt the end, but the Classic Boat Rally carries on - 'a little slower maybe, but no less beautiful'. Predictably, attendance in July 2005 was down somewhat, but it has recovered pretty well. 40 boats attended in 2012, with maybe 90-100 people, despite typically threatening weather. Although speed trials can no longer be held the assembled company cruised to different points round the lake such as Fellfoot, Waterhead and Wray, the Yacht Club and Steamboat Museum. Supper, dinner dance and buffets are hosted in the club in the evenings. The Lakeland Historic Car Club is invited to attend as well, adding

to the vintage ambience, and crews are encouraged to dress the part. The weekend is rounded off by a parade of boats, or Concours d'Elegance, at slow speed past the pier. Prizes are presented to the Commodore's choice.

Speeds are kept low for the whole weekend, but there is evidently a mighty temptation to open up the throttle, unleash that roar and make some waves.

The 2012 entries included 8 Albatross, 4 Delta, 3 Healey, 4 Riva and 2 ChrisCraft, plus the 1948 Knock on Wood which retired with a breakage. All these are inboards.

The British Albatross and Delta runabouts are tiny but characterful, of aluminium sometimes left silver and unpainted. The Healeys are also quite small. The Rivas are really impressive, a peak of 1960s Italian design, all gleaming mahogany and turquoise and white leatherwork; the Ferrari of the waves. These boats have real glamour: Brigitte Bardot sported one at St Tropez. A good throaty roar too from the Chevrolet V8 engine. The firm Riva is going strong, still very Italian and designer, but their present-day boats (the word seems inadequate - floating lifestyle statements is nearer the mark) make the 1960s Junior look very modest. ChrisCraft are also still in production. Their classic boats are similar in size, shape and general style to the Rivas but more American looking, with fins.

The attending boats come from far and wide, including abroad, but a significant proportion are local, belonging to club members.

ABOVE Classic Boat Rally concourse
BELOW Not just classic boats!

STEAM

A rally of steam boats takes place at Broad Leys during a week (Sunday to Friday) in August. Perhaps fifteen or sixteen boats might participate, though it does not generally involve club members. The boats are trailered in, and use the club jetties as a base, paying day membership rates to the club. There are daily cruises to somewhere round the lake, such as Wray castle, picnics, and evening entertainments. It is all quite leisurely. The morning steam-raising, which can take an hour or more, presents a pretty sight, with whiffs of steam, drifts of coal smoke and plenty of mahogany and polished brass in evidence. Steam coal is ordered in bulk specially for the rally. On one day everyone dresses up in Edwardian costume.

These are mostly modern boats however, and quite modest in size - not to be compared with the opulent launches of 1900.

The 1972 International Grand Prix brochure nicely summed up the motorboater's disdain of steam: '... the advantages of which - quietness and smoothness - were outweighed by the disadvantages of having to carry coal, spend time getting up a head of steam, and employ an 'engine driver' to tend all the bulky plumbing which seemed to take up nine-tenths of the boat itself!'

However, steam power does has its own virtues. Particularly pleasing is the moment when each boat finally powers off across the lake; no sound or apparent effort, just a swirl of water round the propeller and faint whisper from the funnel. It is a pleasure too to see these elegant craft slicing through the water in the ideal setting of Windermere and now sharing facilities with powerboat enthusiasts.

BELOW Classic steam boats at the Steamboat Rally

SOCIAL

WMBRC is a flourishing private members' club, the membership reflecting the various water based activities mentioned above. It also has a reputation for fine dining which takes place in the ambiance of this wonderful house. Thus the social side flourishes. The club offers a pretty full social calendar right through the year, from black tie dinner dances to games nights, fancy dress parties to Regatta Balls.

An event of some sort is hosted almost every week. A highlight in August is the Family Week, started by Peter White in 1985, when close to 100 young people enjoy water activities of all sorts. The theme in 2012 was The Olympics, with many water activities, hilarious games, treasure trail and and Olympic fancy dress dinner.

LEFT   Classic steamboats lined up on the Broad Leys' jetties at the Steamboat Rally

THIS PAGE Family Week fun for the young and old.

BELOW   Children's Christmas party

ABOVE   A musical evening at Broad Leys

The boating programme starts with the Fitting Out Dinner in April. This goes back to gentlemanly days when owners employed mechanics to look after and fit out the boats. It was the only time they were invited into the clubhouse, and it could be a somewhat riotous occasion. Now, since the first Lady Commodore, the gathering is mixed and the atmosphere relatively polite.

Fitting Out is followed by a weekend's racing at Barrow. More racing follows in May and every month until October with a Dinner Dance at Broad Leys following each of the three Flag Officers race days . The first major sailing event at the club is the Bénéteau sailing regatta over a weekend in May. There will be a classic boat rally in July, a steam boat rally and family week in August.

A big thank-you dinner for the rescue and patrol boat crews is held in October. The powerboat season winds up with Records Week at Coniston, an international gathering and the only event in the powerboating calendar open to all classes of boat. The K7 Club hold their dinner during that week. The end

LEFT TOP	Laying-up dinner for sailors
ABOVE	Summer evening Croquet
LEFT	Jazz evening on the terrace
BELOW	Jubilee Lunch 2012

of November sees the annual prizegiving at the Hydro Hotel. Christmas and New Year are celebrated with parties and balls which lead into the final days of a year's programme, ending in March but managing to include a Burns night dinner, Valentines' Masked Ball and retiring Commodore's dinner.

These social functions together with external events such as weddings are the funding stream for both powerboat racing and the meticulous upkeep of Broad Leys.

The racing programme and family social programme at WMBRC has developed strong family ties to club racing over many generations

The Lewthwaite family are in the third generation of racing drivers. The late George Lewthwaite was a Commodore, racing driver and friend of Norman H. Buckley. His son Paul and his granddaughter Helen have both raced and attempted records

The late past Commodore Robin Brown raced on Windermere and his son Adam now races at Barrow and has achieved a National record. Robin's father Andrew was Chief Timekeeper for Donald Campbell's last run on Coniston.

Past Commodore and Chairman of House Peter White still races a Phantom at 72 years of age and in 2012 set a new National record on Coniston with a prototype Electric boat. He has three sons Daniel, Philip and Oliver who have all raced, with Daniel being the youngest Commodore of the Club in 2001. George Mould raced with his late first wife Cynthia in the 70s and two of his sons Anthony and Edward took over in the 90s

Philip and Linsey Fairhurst are the children of the late David Fairhurst who raced with George Lewthwaite on Windermere and internationally. Philp started racing in 2012 and Linsey became Peter White's passenger the same year. Philip also achieved a record on Coniston in the same year

Past Commodore Robert Wood, who raced with his brother Richard in the 80s, now has two sons Will and Matthew who race at Barrow. Will is Chairman of the Racing Commitee and his grandfather, Past Commodore James Wood, served for many years as officer of the day controlling race activities on the water with Robin Brown and Richard Solomon to mention but a few.

ABOVE   Wedding at Broad Leys

RIGHT   Sunset dinner in the Broad Leys dining room

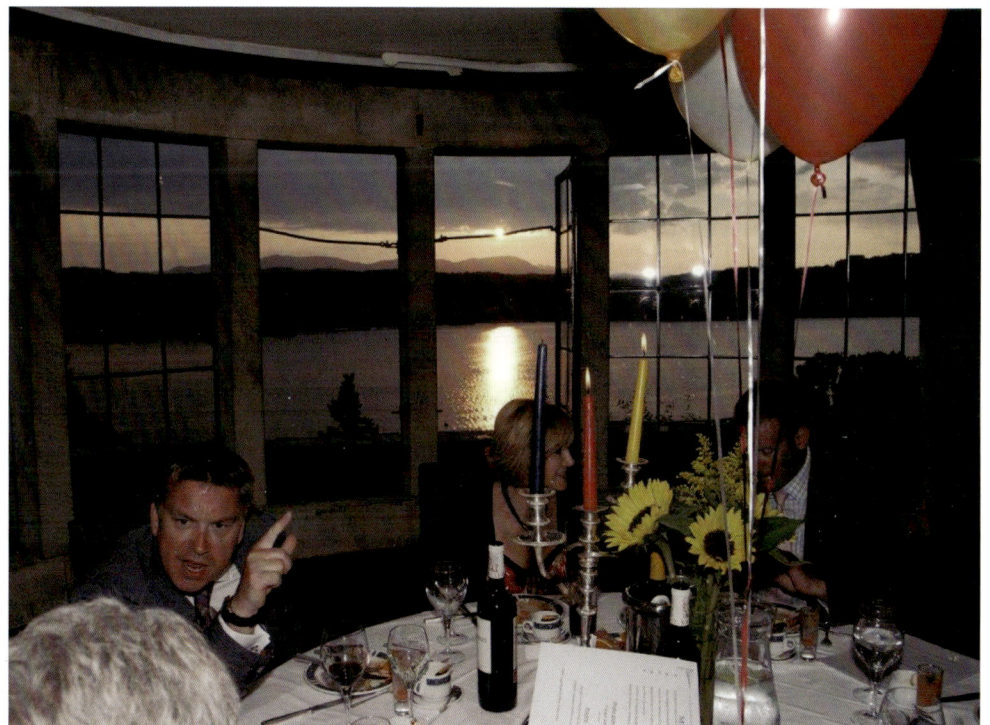

AND SO BACK TO WINDERMERE?

In 2012 a new bylaw was passed giving The Lake District National Park Authority powers to consider, and if appropriate, approve applications for exemption to the speed limit.

The club was delighted to have been granted an exemption and was given permission to bring this long established tradition of powerboat racing back to Windermere for two afternoons in 2013 .

The first of these was the Regatta which took place in mid July 2013. Commodore Lesley Welton noticed a "palpable buzz of excitement in the air" in the build up to the event. Behind the scenes countless people had been frantically working to ensure the occasion was the spectacle it deserved to be. The sun came out and with the patrol crew and rescue team on hand, the racing began. Ten boats were in action and everyone was anxious to see how the first race would go. It went perfectly. All boats finished safely despite the water beginning to resemble the North Sea. Unfortunately the rigours of racing ten

BELOW Afternoon refreshments on the terrace
(All regatta images courtesy of Malcolm Casson Photography)

ABOVE A great place to watch the action from

RIGHT Approaching the finishing line

BELOW Some tricky passing

lap races on a bumpy circuit took its toll and Jim Noone, Will Wood and Julian Rayner all had to retire during the day. However this resulted in the remaining boats benefitting from flatter water The day was all that was hoped for; safe and spectacular. The many spectators, consisting of club members, together with many other lake users watching from the lake, thoroughly enjoyed the day. What could be better than sitting in the sunshine, with picnics and

cream teas whilst watching powerboat racing back on the lake.

The victor on the day was new member Simon Hart in his first season of racing.

The second session of racing on the lake took place at the end of September 2013.

THE CLUB WAS GIVEN PERMISSION TO BRING THIS LONG ESTABLISHED TRADITION OF POWERBOAT RACING BACK TO WINDERMERE FOR TWO AFTERNOONS IN 2013 .

ABOVE *Sheba*, still racing after 40 years

LEFT Commitee members dressed for the occasion

RIGHT Back after 8 years, a catamaran racing on Windermere

BELOW A classic racing boat nicknamed *"the Battleship"*

BROAD LEYS - THE HOUSE

The WMBRC clubhouse, Broad Leys, was in 1970 listed at the highest level at Grade 1: 'One of Voysey's finest houses and one of the most important of its date in Europe'. Caring for such a house is a heavy responsibility. With English Heritage assistance remedial work to the original fabric was carried out, such as new leadwork over the bow windows, repairs to the windows themselves, and stripping off and re-rendering the chimneys. The replacement chimneypots are plain pipes, a sad loss of character from the tapered and bellied pots Voysey had specified.

In 1987-88 it was time for a conservative updating. This was carried out in by Rhodes architects, i.e. Alan Rhodes, who lives in part of Moor Crag. The contractors were G.H. Pattinson, the firm who had built the house in the first place. En-suite showers were added to the main bedrooms. The verandah at the south end of the drawing room had been enclosed in 1950s to make a bar, though the Wisteria prominent in old photographs survives. Now a new

and substantial oak-panelled bar was built within the room; too substantial, perhaps. The fireplace, which had been replaced by one in Cumbrian stone, was reconstructed to Voysey's original pattern, though with new tiles. Not enough of the original irridescent green tiles survived; the replacements are plain and more even dark blue ones. A pencil line indicated the curve of overmantel, so that was reconstructed too. This is the last significant work that has been done at the house.

Broad Leys is Grade 1 listed, implying recognition of architectural merit at the highest level, as well as carrying both restrictions on alteration and the ability to call on funds when serious maintenance or restoration are needed.

Despite the benign preservation of the house as it is there are always unlooked for changes imposed from without. These may be major, e.g. the imposition of a speed limit on the lake, or they may be apparently minor. Such a minor change, which nevertheless has

BROAD LEYS, WAS IN 1970 LISTED AT THE HIGHEST LEVEL AT GRADE 1: 'ONE OF VOYSEY'S FINEST HOUSES AND ONE OF THE MOST IMPORTANT OF ITS DATE IN EUROPE'.

BELOW Terrace at Broad Leys

BELOW IS THE GREAT LAKE, DIFFERENT EVERY DAY AND EVEN FROM HOUR TO HOUR. CALM OR WILD, BALMY OR THREATENING, HEAVENLY BLUE OR STEELY GREY, DARKLY REFLECTIVE OR BRILLIANTLY SPARKLING BY TURNS

a considerable effect on the house, is the banning of incandescent light bulbs. Broad Leys, like Blackwell, had electric light from the beginning. It was in fact essential to the design - gas lighting would have required much higher ceilings to disperse the heat. The effect of incandescent bulbs with Voysey's beautifully warm oak panelling is as effective in its way as candlelight in a Georgian library, and especially at night, when the bow windows throw back curved and seeming infinite reflections of the lights.

To look at a bigger picture, Windermere has proved to be a benign environment for these big houses. So far. A whole string of fine houses, many of them of Arts and Crafts character like Broad Leys, have survived in good shape up and down the lake. As well as Broad Leys, Moor Crag and Blackwell there are Brockhole, Gossel Ridding, Cragwood, Keldwith, Waterbeck and Briery Close as well as the slightly older Pullwoods and Langdale Chase to name a short list. Together they make a gracious and uniquely attractive environment, almost like one big garden.

Very few are still family houses. Some have been divided, some converted to hotels or activity centres. Nevertheless, like Broad Leys, they are much loved and well cared for. The exception, bizarrely enough, is Brockhole, the flagship of the Lake District National Park itself. This is the authority charged with the preservation of the Lake District and its heritage. The house is neglected and has been under threat of demolition, and key features of the garden have been summarily removed. Brockhole and its garden, designed by Dan Gibson and Thomas Mawson, are exactly contemporary with Broad Leys and its degradation and possible loss is an affront to the others.

Broad Leys is in the historic county of Lancashire. The Lancashire / Westmorland boundary is marked on the road immediately outside. We will soon be forgetting that most of the Windermere shoreline, and the whole of the Lake District country round Esthwaite and Coniston, were in Lancashire. It was called Lancashire across the Sands.

First impressions are deceptive. As you sweep into the

LEFT　Two storey great hall

BELOW　Booker committee room in the basement

BOTTOM　An expensive car park!

car park, the house spreads its welcome with its two long and low wings and its harmonious diagonals. The wide front door, usually open, invites you to step inside. A broad and low lobby and cross passage are warm with the rich glow of lightly-oiled oak, and it is only when you emerge into the surprising height of the hall that its full-height bow reveals, almost with a fanfare, a magnificent panorama of the lake. It is a contrived effect, and would have been even more

striking had the early plans for a U-shaped house come to fruition.

There are just three reception rooms, and three principal bedrooms upstairs. It is always worth remembering that this was a holiday house. Arthur and Helen Currer Briggs were very wealthy, with business and civic duties, and would no doubt have been expected to entertain formally and on a lavish

scale back home in Leeds. Broad Leys had a different role, for relaxing and entertaining informally, away from the city. Its architecture reflects this. None of the rooms is particularly big, though the Voysey proportions give them an unusual sense of ease and comfort.

In the middle is the great hall. It is nothing like as grand as it sounds, for the total internal height of the house is only about 16 ft - much lower than the Victorian norm. The idea of breaking down rigid room divisions was highly topical at the time, and the hall is notionally portioned into several parts which were normally allocated separate rooms. There is a sitting area round the big fireplace. A billiard table stood under the porthole window - the mark of the cue rack can be seen, as can the marks of the original light switches, and a corner rack for the balls is still there. A cross corridor, divided off only by two pillars, passes underneath the glazed upper corridor. And the main stair rises graciously off next to the entrance lobby. It sounds complicated but is not. The hall comes into its own today when set out for a big social event, perhaps the Fitting Out Dinner around Easter.

At the north end of the house is the dining room, like the hall hardly changed from 1900. A green-glazed tiled fireplace and more panelling are the salient features, with another bow overlooking the lake and a wide four-light window over the garden. These downstairs rooms are fitted with two-panelled doors and special Voysey door handles and locks. An array of silver cups and trophies are the WMBRC's contribution to the scene, here and in the hall. There is, surprisingly, a single basement room underneath the dining room. It makes use of a declivity in the ground to give it a full window and an external door. This north elevation of the house, seldom seen, is particularly interesting with windows on at least five different levels.

A long corridor leads from the dining room into the service wing. The kitchen, which Rupert Potter photographed in 1912, is a good square room with a big window - Voysey did not believe in hiding the servants away. He has managed to squeeze an attic storey into this wing, and at the far end the floor levels change to give a full three-storey dwelling, all within the same level roofline.

ABOVE Two storey bay window in the great hall

RIGHT Broad Leys dining room

The drawing room at the south end has changed considerably. Rupert Potter's pictures show an elegant square room with double doors out to a south-facing loggia. Light embroidered curtains, a piano, fresh flowers and - intriguingly - the ghostly figure of a lady in black furnish the room. Now the room is no longer square. The verandah has been taken in, making it oblong, and the former piano corner is taken up by a substantial robustly-panelled bar. The original fireplace has gone but has been re-instated, with blue and mechanically-produced tiles in place of the original hand-made green lustre tiles. There is a fitted carpet - which Voysey disliked - and modern sofas, armchairs, and low tables. The club burgee is on the overmantel, photographs of racing boats decorate the walls.

The stair rises, good and wide, in four shallow stages. The four full-height newel posts and the closely-slatted balusters, each one with an inset heart, are eminently typical of the architect. The bannister rails don't slope with the stair, and neither does the broad strip of windows which lights it on three sides. The windowing is exceptionally effective and modern-looking, being set right on the outside plane of the building to be as wide as possible.

Upstairs we have an oak-panelled corridor reaching in a long L round the two wings and articulated by a couple of round arches and the long strip of windows looking down over the hall. The view through the opening windows at night into the cosily lit hall with the black night pressing on the great bow is particularly pleasing. The bedrooms are each fitted with one of Voysey's yellow-tiled fireplaces, and one of his charming air vents appears in each room. The doors, unlike those downstairs, are peasant-style planked doors with latches and strap hinges - but being an Arts and Crafts house the planking is of the finest oak, lightly oiled, the latches have Voysey's heart motif, and the hinge straps are magnificently long. At the angle of the corridor are the two original bathrooms, each tiled in Van Straaten's palest blue tiles and equipped with a massive porcelain bath. The hot taps of the bath still run instantly hot, as specified in 1899.

Out on the terrace the club burgee, the red and white rose on a red, yellow and blue background, flaps on its pole. Below is the great lake, different every day and even from hour to hour. Calm or wild, balmy or threatening, heavenly blue or steely grey, darkly reflective or brilliantly sparkling by turns. What an incredibly beautiful setting for such a magnificent house with such a fascinating history.

WHAT AN INCREDIBLY BEAUTIFUL SETTING FOR SUCH A MAGNIFICENT HOUSE WITH SUCH A FASCINATING HISTORY

APPENDIX

HONORARY MEMBERS:

Earl Howe

Lord Wakefield of Hythe

Sir Henry Segrave

W.G. Dixon

R.B. Stephens

E.H. Pattinson

A.B. Peck

Donald Campbell

I. Wood

J. Whitehead

H.B. Wakefield

R.G. Hornby

A. Roby Jones

Sir John Fisher

His Honour Judge R. Lambert

A.A Brown

K. Evins

G.E. Lewthwaite

T.H. Weir

S.R. Boots

E. Ashworth

V. Humpage

R.G. Brown J.P

R. Solomon

P.M. White

PAST COMMODORES:

Year	Name	Year	Name	Year	Name
1926	E.H. Pattinson	1956	K. Buckley	1986	J.D. Wood
1927	E.H. Pattinson	1957	G.H. Edgecombe	1987	E. Rothwell
1928	E.H. Pattinson	1958	H. Mitchell	1988	J.E.G. Nayler
1929	H.B. Wakefield	1959	F. Astin	1989	H. Addison
1930	J.R. Johnson	1960	C.H. Abbott	1990	K.G. Dervin
1931	J. Whitehead	1961	A.H. Redman	1991	W.J. Bateman
1932	A.B. Peck	1962	R.H. Booker	1992	T. Whitehead
1933	A.C.H. Wilson	1963	S.R. Boots	1993	K.A. Jones
1934	S.S. Nash	1964	H. Gates	1994	S.S. Lewis
1935	E. Milne Eaton	1965	N. Wilson Smith	1995	R.L. Pilkington
1936	Sir Charles W. Craven	1966	R. Hodge	1996	D.G. Brooks
1937	Sir George McKay	1967	Robert E. Smith	1997	P.J. Hill
1938	A. Roby Jones	1968	K. Evins	1998	R.P. Sheperd
1939	E.H. Pattinson	1969	D.N. Haworth	1999	A.T. Lang
1940	E.C.G. Ferreira	1970	H. Wilkinson	2000	D. Greenwood
1941	E.C.F. Ferreira	1971	W. Whatmore	2001	J. Cunliffe
1942	D.C.W. Craven	1972	G. Lambert	2002	D. White
1943	John Village	1973	N.G. Moss	2003	M. Lewis
1944	John Village	1974	V. Humpage	2004	E.Walsh
1945	John Village	1975	G.E.C Nayler	2005	C.M. Walker
1946	John Village	1976	T.H. Weir	2006	J. Hodgen
1947	A. Roby Jones	1977	R.P. Williams	2007	J. Noone
1948	G.R. Morrison	1978	J.H. Davy	2008	A. Whalley
1949	F.B. Lydall	1979	E.Taylor	2009	R.W. Wood
1950	C.V. Haworth	1980	K.P. Taylor	2010	S. McGuffie
1951	J.I. Morrison	1981	N. Cormack	2011	C. Shaw
1952	N.H. Buckley	1982	G.E. Lewthwaite	2012	H. Leung
1953	E.H. Pattinson	1983	R.G. Brown	2013	L. Welton
1954	E.H. Pattinson	1984	M. Smyth		
1955	H. Coop	1985	P.M. White		

TYPICAL CLUB SCHEDULE:

MARCH
Commodore's Cocktail Party
Retiring Commodore's Dinner
AGM Dinner Dance (Black tie)

APRIL
1st Race Day
Easter Egg Hunt & Bar Lunch
Fitting Out Dinner (Black tie)

MAY
1st Sail Day
Rear Commodore's Dinner Dance
Beneteau 21 Sailing Regatta

JUNE
Alfresco Dining
Club Dinner

JULY
Regatta Summer Ball
Lake Cruise
Regatta Golf

AUGUST
Steam Boat Rally
Dinner Dance
Classic Boat Rally
Family Week

SEPTEMBER
Commodore's Dinner Dance
New Members Dinner

OCTOBER
Stock Market Evening

NOVEMBER
Halloween Ball (fancy dress)
Gourmet Dinner
Annual Dinner Dance

DECEMBER
Children's Christmas Party
Christmas Cocktails & Supper
Christmas Lunch
New Year's Eve Ball

JANUARY
Burns Night

FEBRUARY
Chinese New Year Dinner
Valentines Ball
Gourmet Dinner

MEMBERSHIP INFORMATION

If you would like to consider becoming a member and do not know a Club member please apply for a Temporary Member Application Form from our Membership Secretary at the address below .After acceptance as a Temporary member you will be most welcome to any or all of our Social events which will give you an opportunity to see whether you would enjoy becoming Full Member

Broad Leys
Ghyll Head,
Newby Bridge Road
Windermere
Cumbria, LA23 3LJ

Telephone:
015394 43284
Facsimilie:
015394 47004
Email
club@wmbrc.co.uk

WMBRC MEMBERS' WORLD AND NATIONAL RECORDS

These are speed records being the average of consecutive runs over a kilometre unless otherwise specified. W = world record. N = national record.

CLASS	YEAR	RECORD	PILOT	BOAT	ENGINE	SPEED
RACING OUTBOARDS						
O 1000	2011	N	Peter Hart	Hall	Yamaha	66.82
O 2000	2000	W+N	Alan Marshall	Seebold	Mercury	141.39
	2008	W+N	Ted Walsh	DAC	Mercury	144.84
O 3000	2003	N	Ted Walsh	DAC	Mercury	115.79
	2004	W+N				143.90
	2010	W+N				146.89
SPORTS OUTBOARDS						
S 850	1971	N	Nick Huddleston		Konig	53.29
S over 2000	1992	W+N	Tim Whitehead	Burgess	Mercury	105.84
	1998	W+N	Ted Walsh	DAC	Mercury	115.86
One hour	1995	W+N	Alan Marshall	Seebold	Mercury	65.01
S over 2000 monohull	1986	N	Adrian Lang	Phantom	Mercury	76.85
	1989	N	Shahrookh Ardeshir	Blu Fin	Mercury	81.44
	1990	N	Peter Lee	Phantom	Mercury	82.37
S 3000	2006	W+N	Ted Walsh	DAC	Mercury	138.30
RACING INBOARDS						
R 5000	1970	W+N	Norman Buckley	Henderson	Jaguar	111.73
	1972	W+N				114.19
R 7000	1977	W+N	Tony Fahey	Henderson	Jaguar	128.38
R Unlimited	1995	W+N	Jim Noone	Barracuda	Chevrolet	109.85
	1997	W+N				145.52
	2000	W+N				149.16
	2003	W+N				154.77
Formula R 1000	1992	W+N	Jim Noone	Ringwood	Norton	103.47
	2005	N			Polaris	87.01
	2008	N				89.70
	2010	W+N				103.87
900 kgs (KD/800 kgs)	1950	W+N	Norman Buckley	Ventnor	Jaguar	63.49
One hour	1950	W+N				55.55
One hour	1958	W+N		Henderson		89.08
Three hours	1950	W+N		Ventnor		51.58
1200 kgs (KE)	1957	W+N		Henderson		113.57
	1959	W+N				120.63
One hour	1960	W+N				84.83
PRODUCTION OUTBOARDS						
T 850 (T 1, NF, EU)	1988	N	Mike Heaton	Blu Fin	Selva	74.93
	1989	W+N				78.04
	1990	W+N				80.18
NI	1974	N	Nick Huddleston	Levi	Mercury	57.08
NN	1974	N	Richard Solomon	Bristol	Mercury	60.87
NT 6 (Junior)	1986	N	Mike Heaton	Blu Fin	Yamaha	38.25
J 250 (Junior)	2006	N	Nick Walsh	Barnard	Yamaha	40.61
	2008	N		Petarda		43.86
VP 2000	2011	N	Helen Loney	Phantom	Mercury	80.09
VP 2.75	1988	N	Roger Blowers	Phantom	Mercury	82.53
	1989	N				84.13
	2011	N	Chris Loney	Phantom	Mercury	86.60
Mod VP 2.75	1990	N	Tim Whitehead	Hydrostream	Mercury	112.92

ABOVE U11 Unlimited *Namonai* 178mph

(All Record Week images courtesy of Malcolm Casson Photography)

CLASS	YEAR	RECORD	PILOT	BOAT	ENGINE	SPEED
CLUBMAN						
1000 monohull	2010	N	Peter Hart	Wiser	Selva	56.03
	2011	N	Matt Wood	Bristol	Yamaha	56.80
	2012	N	Peter Hart	Vieser	Selva	57.81
1500 monohull	2009	N	Will Wood	Blu Fin	Yamaha	67.68
	2011	N				56.80
2000 monohull	2009	N	Helen Loney	Bernaco	Yamaha	61.93
	2012	N	Helen Loney	Phantom	Mercury	81.03
Unlimited monohull	2005	N	Paul Brooks	Phantom	Mercury	86.09
Frozen 2012	2012	N	Philip Fairhurst	Phantom	Mercury	64.79
		N	Adam Brown	Phantom	Mercury	79.70
		N	Chris Loney	Phantom	Mercury	81.22
1000 catamaran	2011	N	Peter Hart	Hall	Yamaha	60.43
2000 catamaran	2005	N	Paul Scott	Nichols	Mercury	120.00
Unlimited catamaran	2007	N	Helen Loney	DAC	Mercury	100.77
	2008	N	Paul Brooks	DAC	Mercury	128.12
Frozen 2012	2012	N				111.88
FORMULA						
F1 2 litres	1999	W+N	Alan Marshall	Seebold	Mercury	136.74
	2000	W+N				139.97
F1 2.5 litres	2002	W+N	Alan Marshall	Seebold	Mercury	145.90
F1 3 litres	2001	W+N	Alan Marshall	Seebold	Mercury	131.54
F2	1999	W+N	Ted Walsh	DAC	Mercury	122.91
	2000	W+N				124.08
	2001	W+N				124.69
One hour	2000	W+N				74.01
	2001	W+N				77.99
Two hours		W+N				76.70
Three hours	2000	W+N				70.39
F3	2001	W+N	Paul Scott	Burgess	Evinrude	99.65
	2003	W+N		Hung ASV	Johnson	100.69
F3000	2007	N	Chris Loney	DAC	Mercury	100.70
	2008	N				130.92
RIB						
R2	2012	N	Peter Hart	Mannerfelt	Mercury	77.63
ELECTRIC						
48 volts	2008	N	Helen Loney	Danisch	Agni	13.80
72 volts	2009	N	Helen Loney	Danisch	Agni	21.08
Unrestricted	2012	N	Peter White			32.77
OUTRIGHT						
Outboard immersed prop	2002	N	Alan Marshall	Seebold	Mercury	145.90
Inboard immersed prop	1970	N	Norman Buckley	Borwick	Jaguar	113.74
	1977	N	Tony Fahey	Borwick	Jaguar	128.38
	1997	N	Jim Noone	Barracuda	Chevrolet	145.52
	2000	N				149.16
	2003	N				154.77
Three hours	1966	W+N	Norman Buckley	Borwick	Jaguar	75.96
Outboard immersed prop monohull	2005	N	Mike Horn	Phantom	Mercury	78.33
	2006	N	Paul Brooks	Phantom	Mercury	86.92
Electric	2005	W+N	Helen Loney	Campbell	Agni	68.09
	2008	W+N		Ringwood		76.80
Ladies	2008	N	Helen Loney	DAC	Mercury	125.80